MW00588402

CRISIS and LEADERSHIP

By Clara Fraser
and Richard Fraser

RED LETTER PRESS • SEATTLE

© 2000 by Red Letter Press
409 Maynard Avenue South, Suite 201
Seattle, WA 98104 ● (206) 682-0990
RedLetterPress@juno.com
All rights reserved
Printed in the United States of America

Revised Edition 2000

Book and cover design: Helen Gilbert
Notes: Tamara Turner

The present work was first published in 1965 as two
internal bulletins of the Socialist Workers Party.
Part One was reissued in 1969 as *Crisis and Leadership*
by Freedom Socialist Publications, Seattle.
Part Two appeared in 1977 in two installments of the
Freedom Socialist newspaper (Vol. 3, nos. 1 and 2)
as "Radical Laborism versus Bolshevik Leadership:
The Organization Problem of the Socialist Workers Party."

Library of Congress Cataloging-in-Publication Data

Fraser, Clara, 1923-
    Crisis & leadership / by Clara Fraser and Richard Fraser.
        p.   cm.
    Rev. ed. of: Crisis and leadership / Richard Kirk. 1969-
    Includes bibliographical references and index.
    ISBN 0-932323-08-1 (pbk. : alk. paper)
        1. Radicalism—United States. 2. Socialism—
    United States. 3. Socialist Workers Party.
    4. Afro-Americans—Civil rights—History—20th century.
    5. Women and socialism—United States.
    6. United States—Social conditions—1960-1980.
    7. United States—Social conditions—1980-
    I. Title: Crisis and leadership. II. Fraser, Richard S.,
    1913-1988. III. Kirk, Richard, 1913-1988. Crisis and
    leadership. IV. Title.

    HN90.R3 F74 2000
    322.4'4'0973—dc21   00-27348

Contents

Introduction to the 2000 Edition

I first read *Crisis and Leadership* nearly 25 years ago as a newcomer to radical politics, part of a generation zapped to consciousness by the Vietnam War, the 1968 student revolts, and Black civil rights insurgency. What an eye-opener this document was for someone swept up in that frenetic time!

The '60s were a social maelstrom with new upheavals—political, economic, and technological—erupting weekly. The New Left dominated the dissident scene. Brash, raucous, and fiercely anti-theoretical, it rejected voices of experience for the flashpoint slogan "Do It Now!" The problem was that few of us had a clue what a worthwhile "It" might be, let alone what "It" would accomplish, or what would come next.

The lucid analysis of *Crisis and Leadership* injected clarity into those murky waters. From its pages, I gained a better understanding of the debates of that heady time and found a scientific basis for my strong but vague sense that something must be fundamentally wrong with a system that spawned misery everywhere around the world.

From *Crisis and Leadership*, I learned that capitalism, the economic system of the U.S. and much of the world, inevitably foments war. I discovered that racism is not an *aberration* in the "land of the free," but an intrinsic part of this country's social structure. I gained a vivid sense of the momentous choices facing the African American freedom struggle. And I developed a keener understanding of the seminal role people of color must play in the battle to revolutionize U.S. society.

As a passionate feminist, I was thrilled to see that the

authors took the "Woman Question" out of an auxiliary, tag-along status and placed it smack in the center of the fight against all other oppressions. This was extremely fore-sighted, considering the document was written before the term "women's lib" was coined, before Stokely Carmichael made his infamous declaration that "the position of women in the movement is prone," and at a time when, in even the most progressive circles, women made coffee but never policy!

For me and others who came of age as rebels in that era, *Crisis and Leadership* was a crucial first exposure to a rational, radical program and course of action for sweeping, humanistic social change. It linked us to the historical development of socialist thought and introduced us to the ideas of Leninism and Trotskyism. I learned that the essence of these much-maligned "isms" is a disciplined party, a program of workers democracy and internationalism, and a fierce commitment to truthful and principled revolutionary politics.

A wake-up call for the moribund SWP

Crisis and Leadership, like many of the great texts of Marxism, was polemical in origin, the product of a sharp controversy on the Left. It was written for the 1965 convention of the Socialist Workers Party (SWP) by Richard Fraser (Kirk) and Clara Fraser (Kaye), on behalf of what was known as the Kirk-Kaye Tendency, which comprised the entire Seattle branch of the SWP and had numerous supporters in other cities. ("Kirk" and "Kaye" were pseudonyms adopted because of the intense harassment of radicals by government and employers during the McCarthy period. Clara Fraser, for example, was hounded from job to job by the FBI for over a decade. Using aliases was a common and necessary practice in the socialist movement at that time.)

The Kirk-Kaye Tendency was a loyal, hard-working internal opposition that successfully organized for the SWP on every front while conducting a decade-long battle to return the party to the interventionist and explicitly revolu-

6

tionary course from which it had strayed. The fundamental question was whether radicals should disguise their politics and follow the masses—or lead, using transitional demands to educate for socialism. The minority's disagreements centered on policy and tactics on issues concerning African Americans, women, labor, the antiwar movement, and international affairs. *Crisis and Leadership* details these and other differences with the party majority led by Farrell Dobbs and Tom Kerry.

The Socialist Workers Party had drastically declined since its heyday in the 1930s and '40s when it was the flagship of world Trotskyism. The early SWP had been an inspiring prototype of a revolutionary party. It was skillfully steered by James P. Cannon and benefited immensely from the guidance of Leon Trotsky himself. Integrating theory and action, the party led labor uprisings and heroically opposed the imperialist agenda in World War II. It was a recognized and respected defender of Black civil rights during the 1940s; by 1948 almost half the party was African American. During the '50s, however, under pressure from McCarthyism and the increasingly conservative trade unions to which the party oriented, the SWP began a downhill slide from its proud traditions. A huge exodus of Black members took place around 1950 as a result of the anticommunist witch-hunts and the SWP's confusing and contradictory approach to the Black movement.

Crisis and Leadership crowned the Kirk-Kaye Tendency's ten-year effort to reverse the party's erosion. It was originally published as two companion documents. Part One, entitled "The Crisis" in this book, was a Political Resolution—an assessment of the international and domestic situation put before the membership for adoption at a party convention. The Kirk-Kaye Resolution was offered as a substitute to the Political Resolution proposed by the SWP Political Committee at the party's 1965 National Convention. Though Clara and Richard Fraser were the primary authors, the document was a collective effort on the part of the entire Seattle branch and co-thinkers in San Francisco, Detroit, Los Angeles, Chicago, New York, and Connecticut. Clara Fraser gave particular acknowledgment to African American comrade Waymon (Skip) Ware for his contributions to the section on the Black movement.

Part Two, called "Leadership" in this volume, was published under the title "Radical Laborism versus Bolshevik Leadership: The Organization Problem of the Socialist Workers Party" as a pre-convention Discussion Bulletin (Vol. 25, No. 14) for the same SWP convention. It scrupulously diagnoses the degenerated condition of the party's leadership bodies, activities, and general health. It shows that the SWP's organizational deterioration, which included an alarming constriction of party democracy, was linked to its failure to rise to changed political realities in the world at large.

The Kirk-Kaye Political Resolution was rejected by the convention with virtually no opportunity for rank-and-file consideration. Even worse, the convention passed a measure that outlawed internal factions, ending the tendency's hopes of influencing the party majority.

In early 1966, Clara Fraser was kicked off the SWP National Committee. The party regime whipped up a campaign of censure, slander and harassment of the tendency's supporters. By the spring of '66, the faction was forced to conclude that remaining in the party would mean political death.

On April 9, 1966, the entire Seattle branch and its supporters nationally formally resigned from the SWP in order to build a new party that would keep revolutionary Trotskyism alive and responsive to the demands of a new era. *Crisis and Leadership* became the theoretical cornerstone of a bold new formation, the Freedom Socialist Party (FSP).

A time-tested analysis

Revisiting *Crisis and Leadership* today, I am struck by its insightful predictions and pertinence for contemporary radicals. To see its thoroughly Marxist analysis vindicated by time is all the more impressive, considering we are judging it in light of profound and sometimes devastating changes on the world scene, most notably the collapse of the Soviet Union.

The USSR's fall forced many radicals to confront the failure of Stalinism. But some overreacted and turned their backs on socialist fundamentals as well. Others became disheartened and demoralized. In contrast, *Crisis and Leadership* shows that Marxism remains the only tool for getting to the root of today's problems and vanquishing them.

By examining five key components of *Crisis and Leadership,* we can judge how its analysis stacks up after 30 years. These issues are the condition of U.S. capitalism, the increasingly repressive role of the state, the choices facing the workers states, the rise of fascism, and the political degeneration of the SWP.

Capitalist economic malaise

Crisis and Leadership was written after more than a decade of relative prosperity, while the "Great Society" of President Lyndon Johnson was still building steam. Yet it forecast an economic meltdown comparable in severity to the Great Depression, although quite different in form.

The authors characterized the coming crisis as deep and abiding. But they also predicted that the ruling class would better protect itself than in the past—and would do so at the cruel expense of working people, especially people of color and women. They anticipated that the state would play a more overt role in bolstering big corporations and smashing labor and social movements. And they expected that increased competition for profitable investments would escalate tensions between the U.S. and non-capitalist and colonial nations, resulting in stepped-up American intervention to crush rebellion around the world.

The last 30 years show these projections to be right on.

The U.S. has endured a series of recessions, each leaving, as the authors state, "a residue of unemployment and poverty." Since the late '80s, corporate profits have soared, but the vaunted upturn never trickled down to working people and the poor. To the contrary, big business continues "downsizing," and laid-off workers are never rehired. Real wages have fallen steadily, widening the gap between rich and poor. And despite rosy claims of low unemployment, large numbers of discouraged workers have permanently deserted the job market; many others are *under*-employed. Masses of young people, especially youth of color, have few prospects.

Repressive role of the state

As foretold in 1965, the state is putting ever-increasing weight into shoring up the bosses.

The U.S. government subsidizes big business through many ploys old and new, from tax credits and open corporate welfare to privatizing social services. But the state does not limit its role to stacking the economic deck. When necessary, it uses its armed might against any opposition to the status quo.

Within a few years of the writing of *Crisis and Leadership*, violent repression rained down against the very sector the authors had identified as the greatest potential threat to the system: the revolutionary wing of the Black movement.

The police and FBI systematically jailed or assassinated nearly the entire leadership of the Black Panther Party during the '70s. In addition, the American Indian Movement (AIM) was ravaged by violent frame-ups and sabotage. These assaults were part of the government's notorious COINTELPRO (counterintelligence program), which subjected organizations of radicals and people of color to intense levels of spying, "disinformation" campaigns, and internal disruption.

In the following decade, the Reagan and Bush administrations declared war against labor. The 1980s commenced with the federal government bludgeoning the strike of 12,000 air-traffic controllers.

Repression has not been limited to the home front. Around the world, wherever rebels confront imperialism, or multinational corporations fear for their profits, the U.S. government intervenes. Economic coercion, covert support of reactionary forces and limited or threatened military deployment may do the trick, as in Nicaragua. If not, the U.S. accelerates to full-scale assault and invasion, as was the case in Grenada, Panama, Somalia, Iraq and Yugoslavia.

The workers states

At the time *Crisis and Leadership* was written, China and Cuba were wellsprings of revolutionary inspiration. By overthrowing capitalism, they had defied the Stalinized USSR's choke-hold on world revolution. The drama of the world's most afflicted rising up to victory sent tremors through the Communist and Socialist parties of Europe, sparked insurgency all over Asia, Africa and Latin America, and resonated among U.S. youth.

Today we face a far different situation, but one which *Crisis and Leadership* is still invaluable in explaining. The pressures from world capitalism and Stalinism that the authors describe have forced China and Cuba into dangerous "free market" experiments and have wrought the downfall of the USSR.

Unrelenting hostility from the West combined with the anger of workers over decades of Stalinist repression and economic mismanagement brought down the world's first workers state and Stalinist bureaucracies throughout the Eastern Europe.

During the ensuing years, capitalism has savaged these former workers states and reintroduced the naked exploitation, piracy, and nationalistic rivalries of the early Industrial Revolution. But "free enterprise" is far from triumphant, especially in Russia where the effort to reimpose capitalism has so far proved an unmitigated disaster. There is every hope that the people of the ex-workers states will develop fresh revolutionary leadership and once again renounce capitalism for socialism, particularly if animated by political revolt in the U.S. and other industrialized countries.

In the case of China, the authors of *Crisis and Leadership* were optimistic, because China had avoided "both the economic pitfalls of Stalinist misrule and the political degeneration accompanying it." Hope for the revolution's continued progress was warranted by China's internationalism and its break with the disastrous Stalinist doctrine of peaceful co-existence with imperialism. Since then, however, China has reversed course on all these fronts, while still not descending to the nadir of repression and bureaucratic counterrevolution reached in the USSR. Today, private industry is making serious inroads in China, and while the foundations of the workers state still exist, the revolution's fate is balanced on a knife's edge.

Cuba's revolution has been the most durable. Amid merciless U.S. siege, it is still, to quote *Crisis and Leadership*, "a permanent dagger pointed at the heartland of imperialism." However, it has retreated from open support and aid to uprisings and national liberation struggles around the world, dangerously increasing its isolation. To compensate for the loss of subsidies from the USSR, risky market-based and foreign investment strategies have been introduced. Dependence on U.S. dollars is creating an inequality of wealth not seen since the revolution, and government food subsidies are not staving off hunger. On the positive side, the CP-led government has retained the people's loyalty by becoming more responsive to popular demands, notably from women and lesbian/gay activists. The revolution is holding on to its commitment to socialism.

The choices which *Crisis and Leadership* outlined for the workers states—socialist internationalism and proletarian democracy or reversion to imperialist domination—are still the choices they face today.

Growth of fascism

Crisis and Leadership theorized that capitalism's global crisis would impel the ruling powers rightward. The authors saw signs that the Southern Ku Klux Klan was courting the Northern far-right with the goal of establishing a police state to level workingclass opposition.

Today, we have indeed witnessed a rise in the violent ultra-right, a phenomenon tolerated and surreptitiously encouraged by the bourgeoisie. They hold the neo-Nazis at arm's length, ready for the day when only a fascist solution can save their profit system.

That day is not yet here and hopefully never will be, since, as was also predicted, the economic crisis is inciting radicalization too.

Women, people of color, lesbians and gays, and young people are increasingly on the move, leading key labor and social battles. They are sparking renewed rank-and-file offensives against cautious movement figureheads and business-as-usual union bureaucrats. And in a historic development, a labor party has been formed in the U.S. —though it is yet to be determined whether it will break with the Democratic Party and become a truly independent voice for workers.

Though the right wing is a clear and present danger, all signs indicate tremendous potential for a giant leap forward that will send it scurrying for cover.

The SWP withers

Thirty years after the Kirk-Kaye Tendency judged the SWP to have turned away from the revolutionary road, that organization has fulfilled their direst expectations. Its deficiencies—fixation on the most conservative union sectors, tailending of the Black movement, resistance to women's revolutionary potential, intolerance of dissident viewpoints, and ossified bureaucratism—have proved fatal although the corpse still walks among us.

Far from being ancient history, the reasons for the SWP's demise are of the greatest relevance for left groups today—most of which are still grappling with the very same issues.

The waning of the '60s mass protests accelerated the degeneration of the SWP's program, actions and organizational norms. It retreated from even token interest in people of color and women, intensifying its "laborite" orientation to the union aristocracy of higher paid, more privileged workers. SWP National Secretary Jack Barnes proclaimed, "We are not going to see the development of some sort of nonwhite or nonmale vanguard,"[1] and members trooped obediently into heavy industry in search of the "real" working class.

Unsurprisingly, during the '70s and early '80s, the SWP experienced waves of splits and sweeping expulsions. Large numbers of activists dropped out. The breakdown of the U.S. party was mirrored in sympathizing organizations around the world.

Hoping to revitalize themselves by grabbing the coattails of the Cuban and the short-lived Grenadan revolutions, the SWP and its affiliates went so far as to explicitly renounce Trotskyism. The party now does little more than play an opportunist but mostly insignificant role in Cuba support work and run embarrassingly perfunctory electoral campaigns.

Since the '70s, no tendency that left or was forced out of the SWP has formulated a serious analysis of the party's derailment. The new opposition groups merely replicate the diseased politics described in *Crisis and Leadership*. They may kvetch over the particular issue that led to their disenchantment or disfavor, but none question the basic orientation that led the SWP astray. For this reason, none has become a vital revolutionary force.

FSP—a going concern

It's great for a critic to be proven right—but can she or he do better? That Clara Fraser and her comrades did!

Unlike any recent dissidents to exit the SWP (or the Communist Party, for that matter), the Kirk-Kaye Tendency did something quite brave and brazen—they set out to build an authentic Bolshevik party, and they succeeded. Though Richard Fraser and others defected a year later when they found they had to walk their talk on the Woman Question, the FSP majority created an unprecedented new organism—a revolutionary Leninist, socialist feminist party.

From its nucleus in Seattle, Washington, the Freedom Socialist Party has taken root in a number of U.S. cities with sympathizing sections in Canada and Australia. It has a remarkable record of accomplishments—from leading strikes, to waging courtroom battles against discrimination and McCarthyism, to confronting Nazis toe-to-toe. FSP has distinguished itself on the Left for its profound integration of socialism and feminism, its emphasis on the necessary leadership role of people of color and national minorities in the worldwide class struggle, and its defense of lesbian/gay rights as an issue of first-rank importance. The party's early history is told in *A Victory for Socialist Feminism* and *Socialist Feminism: The First Decade, 1966-76*.[2] FSP's sister organization, Radical Women, offers workingclass women an alternative to single-issue feminist reformists, intervenes in every arena, and has published numerous theoretical writings.

In a world that is today even more caustically anti-party than during the height of the New Left, the development and achievements of the FSP demonstrate why a democratic, principled revolutionary party is vital for people who are serious about changing the world. Perhaps even more important, the FSP proves such a party can exist!

Crisis and Leadership today

As we enter the 21st century, the analysis offered by

Crisis and Leadership is more timely and meaningful than ever. U.S. radicals and Trotskyists everywhere need to know and understand our movement's history, origins, and errors in order to advance. This book makes that much easier by publishing the two components of *Crisis and Leadership* together for the first time and providing expanded notes and related documents that give further context and information on the Freedom Socialist Party's formation and ideas. For the sake of readability, some very minor editorial revisions have also been made to the text.

The Left must understand why the SWP failed if it is to master the contradictions of a capitalist system in crisis, maintain equilibrium amid the collapse of the Soviet Union, and effectively confront the growing right wing. We urgently need the critical thinking, bold ideas, innovative strategies and dauntless model of an effective revolutionary organization represented in these pages.

SUSAN WILLIAMS, M.D.
New York, New York

Introduction to the 1969 Edition

A growing number of partisans of the Black liberation and antiwar struggles in the United States have come to the conclusion that only revolutionary change in the basic structure of the society will bring any progress.

This is not exactly a new idea. It has a hundred-year history back to Karl Marx' articles in the *New York Tribune* supporting the antislavery cause in the Civil War. However, the two organizations today which most "officially" represent a Marxist revolutionary tradition have done little to win the respect of radicals. Both the Communist Party (CP) and the Socialist Workers Party (SWP), after years of little accomplishment, have claimed dogmatically to be correct on all questions as a matter of doctrine. At the same time each has played a conservative role in the development of radicalism in the movement.

It is small wonder that new radicals have thus looked upon the Old Left as dead and better forgotten. The endless polemics conducted by the Old Left seem detached, obscure, and unrelieved by a parallel record of struggle. It would, of course, be inaccurate to say that the New Left *initiated* the past period of mass struggle. Rather, the new radical forces are a *product* of the mass protest. They have, however, established an enviable record of personal valor. The nation's jails are full of Black militants. Thousands of youth, Black and white, have defied the draft and faced unrestrained police savagery in demonstrations.

Years of mass demonstrations and rebellion have occurred, however, and everything remains the same. Peace and Black liberation seem as distant as ever. Federal legislation on civil rights is a sham. Both parties have nominated hawks for the presidency. A bloody conspiracy involving unknown forces in the power structure decides which national leaders live and die. The peaceful mass demonstrations have dropped off. What did they accomplish? There is today, combining with the activism of physical protest, a more reflective mood. In this circumstance, it is on the order of the day for those newly committed to the idea of basic social change to consider that perhaps there is more to learn from the past than appears on the surface.

Hans Enzensberger, on leaving the U.S. to live in Cuba, wrote, "I believe the class which rules the United States of America, and the government which implements its policies, to be the most dangerous body of men on earth."[3] Dangerous, yes, but also skilled in the art of ruling society and dictating the course of a large part of the world. These men do not eschew theory or act blindly. On the contrary, although in the last analysis they rely on the naked power of the police and military, they enlist universities full of experts in every field and have at their disposal all of the techniques and media for persuasion by delicate means as well as by terror.

In addition, they have the whole weight of tradition and social inertia and conservatism on their side.

No one who has a serious bone in his body would attempt to mount a force to overthrow this power without an exhaustive effort to understand the nature of the political and economic forces that operate in American capitalist society. In this light, the polemics that have engaged the Old Left all these years might seem less irrelevant.

For a movement to throw itself blindly against the naked power of the American profit system, protected by its police and military, on the bare strength of its faith in the justice of its cause, is just as futile as the decades of conclaves in attic headquarters over "when our day comes."

On reflection, however, neither process is futile. Every assault on an armory, a barricaded street, or the Pentagon need not be a military victory. Experience is required to learn tactics, and setbacks can be valuable lessons as well as defeats.

However, a movement progresses on the basis of the past. If every generation has to learn everything all over again, it is hard to exceed the accomplishments of the last generation. A great deal of genuine revolutionary effort has gone into determining the nature of capitalist society in our era of imperialism, and the nature of American society in particular with its peculiar institution of race relations. The new generation of radicals would do well to review the debates of the past because they concerned the life and death questions of today.

The decline of elements of the past movement does not erase the validity of efforts at an earlier time. Today's movement would do well, for instance, to learn from the Communist Party of the '20s and the Socialist Workers Party of later years the art of mass public defense of victims of police prosecution. The courts are having a field day today jailing militants. Protest and picket lines are not enough. It is necessary to enlist the sympathetic support of millions not yet ready to fight, but willing to defend the rights of others to do so! Such support has been marshaled successfully in the past.

Of all the older movements, none took a more serious approach to the understanding of society as a basis for action than the Socialist Workers Party. The SWP maintained the continuity of revolutionary thought and action through a period of great difficulty. The decades encompassing the Second World War and the witch hunt which followed were hardly characterized by mass movements in the streets. SWP leaders at first, and CP leaders later, served prison sentences following Smith Act convictions.[4]

From 1940 to 1960 a whole generation of youth was raised in a period of relatively slow struggle. Although not altogether correct, it is nevertheless understandable that radical youth of today often say they will not listen to anyone over 30. They are excluding the lost generation. Elements of that generation, however, maintained revolutionary continuity under adverse conditions. Such elements were largely in the SWP. In fact, the SWP produced a generation of personally devoted and talented revolutionaries. This is not erased by the latter day decline of the SWP. It was hardly ordained by history that any group could maintain a consistent and correct policy for a quarter of a century without a major breakthrough.

The relevancy of the decline of the SWP today depends on one's view of the nature of the problem of leadership in a period of revolutionary change. The New Left operates largely on the working assumption that leadership springs out of activity at the time needed. It is an interesting contradiction that these same people often accuse Marx of proposing an automatic, economistic view of history. On the contrary, Marxism holds that historical problems in general will not resolve themselves, and that in particular the creation of a rational society out of capitalist chaos and brutality in America will not occur automatically.

From this view has come the struggle of the Old Left to create a long-range professional leadership, an absolutely necessary step if the developing sectional and transitory struggles are to be integrated into a serious fight for power.

As it became obvious that the SWP was no longer filling the requirement, many of its supporters reorganized. Among these was a group in Seattle with some supporters elsewhere who had fought a long 15-year fight within the SWP against the process of degeneration. They joined with other socialists in Seattle to form the Freedom Socialist Party.

Two of the leaders who had left the SWP to form the FSP, Richard Kirk and Clara Kaye, wrote the article which follows. They exemplified the best tradition of personal integrity and spirit which had developed in the SWP. Although over the years their differences with the SWP central leadership developed around a number of questions, the central dispute was over the question of Black liberation.

The SWP had traditionally considered the question of race relations basically to be a *national* question, similar to if not identical with the question of Eastern Europe in relation to Russia. But the fight for Black liberation had a history of its own, older than the Russian Revolution, and a study of this history indicated that the race question was independent of nationality and had special social laws. A correct understanding of this question may be crucial in an effort to overthrow the profit system. Racial oppression is at one and the same time irrational and anachronistic and yet an integral part of the fabric of our society. It is a fatal flaw in the otherwise solid appearing wall of capitalist power.

The SWP failed to appreciate the nature of this question although Kirk and Kaye attempted to correct the policy. As the years went by, the conservatism that was growing in the SWP blinded it also to a correct view on many other questions: China, women's emancipation, party democracy, etc.

In 1965 Kirk and Kaye wrote the following article as a summary of their criticism and position. It was proposed to the SWP convention that year as a resolution and was rejected. It comprised the political ground upon which the Seattle group left a few months later.

A three-year-old minority convention document of an obscure leftwing party may seem to the average reader of 1968 a trifle esoteric. But people concerned with revolutionary change ought to develop the practice of exchanging views and treating each other seriously. Anyway, how many supposed revolutionaries wrote anything in 1965 they are willing to see published today? Is it worthwhile? The reader will have to judge for himself.

DAVID DREISER[5]
New Haven, Connecticut

Note on terminology: This book reflects the swift changes during the 1960s in how African Americans described themselves. The authors originally used the term "Negro," because at the time they were writing this was standard usage in the Black community. When Part One was publicly issued in 1969, the editors updated it with the new term "Black." We have retained that usage in the main body of the text. However, for historical accuracy we have not revised the terminology in the documents in the appendices.

Part 1
The Crisis

The international dilemma

Factors of the crisis

The radical movement in the United States stands at a crossroads.

World capitalism is in a fundamental crisis. The southern Black revolt is stirring the world. China is realigning the old Third International against the Kremlin.[6] Cuba steadfastly defends its heroic revolution. And newly radicalized currents opposed to government policies are emerging in the U.S., created and buoyed up by the Black revolt and the antiwar movement, counterbalanced by a growing and nationally unified fascist movement and a mounting Bonapartism in the state.

All these phenomena telegraph the imminence of a *pre-revolutionary* situation in the United States.

The need and the opportunity coexist today for the most significant regroupment and coalescence of revolutionary vanguard forces since the formation of the Communist Party after the Russian Revolution. The forces providing this opportunity emanate from the world crisis of capitalism which comprises four key factors:

The end of the postwar boom. The lack of new opportunities for capital investment is bringing to a close the post-World War II economic upsurge which was powered by the replacement of fixed capital destroyed or made obsolescent by 15 years of depression and war.

The proletarian stage of the colonial revolution. After the first waves of the postwar colonial revolutions placed the colonial bourgeoisie in power, today in Asia, Latin America and Africa, the proletariat demonstrates the Permanent Revolution in life, tearing strategic politico-economic sectors out of the imperialist orbit.[7]

The death-throes of European reformism. The convulsions within the Socialist and particularly the Communist parties—the key props of European capitalism—foretell their disintegration and the arrival of the proletariat at the threshold of revolutionary politics.

The emerging revolution in the U.S. South. Currently creating vast turmoil in U.S. politics, the Black movement is capable of paralyzing the government and inspiring sympathetic demonstrations of a revolutionary nature here and abroad.

These four main symptoms of the coming international showdown between reaction and socialism expose the severity of the crisis and provide the global backdrop for the intricate socio-economic-political drama now unfolding in the U.S.

Political economy of the crisis

Since World War II, world capitalist economy has experienced an upswing of extraordinary duration in the main imperialist centers: Western Europe, Japan and the United States.

The protracted boom, lasting for the better part of two decades, had its origins in intrinsic laws of capitalism, but its course has been sustained by the concerted intervention of the state into the national economy, particularly in the U.S., reflecting the advanced stage of monopolistic imperialism.

The boom

The obsolescence, decay and outright physical obliteration wrought by a decade-and-a-half of worldwide depression and war effectively destroyed a large part of the fixed capital of the capitalist world, creating a heavy demand for capital investment. This condition was the fundamental force bolstering the postwar upswing.

The mere need for fixed capital replacement assured that an economic rise would take place, provided, of course, the political situation could be stabilized and that sufficient capital could be mobilized for the initial investment thrust.

In addition, capitalism had at its disposal a vast accumulation of technical innovations, some of which had lain dormant during the great depression, but were production-tested in the massive imperialist war machines. These innovations laid the basis for the creation of whole new industries and technical revolutions in others. This chain of effects once set in motion was sufficient to engender a prolonged recovery.

Until the last three or four years, American prosperity has been marred by slow growth and several short-cycle recessions. The accelerated rate of growth in certain industries since 1962, which has imparted some of the feverishness of the classic capitalist boom to the U.S. economy, indicates not that American capitalism has solved its problems, but that a rapid accumulation of contradictions is underway, fomenting future explosions.

While the prosperity has been very real for the bourgeoisie, broad layers of the middle class and a considerable section of the working class, each recovery has left a substantial residue of unemployment, and expanding areas of poverty have accumulated.

American capital has been frantically attempting to regain its unchallenged hegemony in the world market. The recent wave of investments has been largely concentrated on introducing lower-cost production techniques calculated to place U.S. capital in a better competitive position, for its relatively declining share of the world market threatens to turn into an absolute decline.

Europe has served as a major market for American goods and capital, and the receding of its boom denotes an imminent constriction of investment opportunities there. Particularly ominous for American capital is the growing friction with its European partners. European capitalists, feeling the squeeze from American subsidies and from outright American acquisition of native industries, are beginning to pressure their governments for assistance. At a time when the international exchange position of the dollar depends on co-operative European governments, this antagonism is serious.

The revival of imperialist rivalries among World War II allies and enemies alike (U.S., Western Europe, Britain, Japan) has generated new frictions in the capitalist world, and both Great Britain and the U.S. have suffered persistent negative balance of international payments since the late '50s.

The crisis in realizing profits

One, or several, of the monetary and secondary economic problems *could* trigger a crisis. However, short of a general capitalist crisis, monopoly capitalism possesses sufficient economic controls to minimize the effect of secondary contradictions, provided that relative political equilibrium can be maintained. It is within the domain of the *basic* laws of capital that the primary contradictions of the system take shape. Here exist the elements that predetermine crisis for the system as a whole, and it is here, in fact, that the basic conditions for a coming general crisis are being shaped.

The postwar boom has depended ultimately on the normal recuperative forces of capitalism, but these forces are inherently limited. The process of new capital construction is far advanced and the point must eventually be reached when the need to realize profits from existing fixed capital will come into decisive conflict with the urge toward new investment. The enormous capital investment generated by the boom, demanding realization, indicates that no resolution of this conflict is possible other than a general crisis affecting all the major world capitalist centers.

Recent changes in the economic conjuncture concretely indicate the drift toward crisis. Most Western European nations have had full employment for several years, but this was accompanied by a general downward trend of profits plus marked tendencies toward inflation. Also, chronic excess capacity has appeared in several basic industries, and in recent months real manufacturing recessions have occurred in France, Great Britain and Japan.

In the U.S., the wave of heavy investment that produced the first real boom in this country since the end of the Korean War in 1953 continues to absorb great quantities of capital and manpower, but close observers note a downward trend in appropriations for capital outlays.

These signs all point in the same direction: toward a general realization crisis. While it is impossible to give a precise timetable for the evolution of the crisis, it is clear that it must be soon, perhaps within months, certainly within a very few years.

When the crisis does mature, it cannot have any other than a deep and abiding character, due to the very magnitude of the postwar recovery and the corresponding velocity of the downward drag exerted by the huge amount of fixed investments. Moreover, no matter where the crisis first appears in decisive form, no country, including this one, can long escape it; the close interdependence of European nations, and the heavy concentration of American capital there, insure it.

The brewing crisis of capitalism has all the potential of a depression on the scale of that during the 1930s, but there are good reasons to believe that the crisis will *not assume the same form*.

After the 1929 crash, the bourgeoisie as a whole was stunned and paralyzed, incapable of decisive action for several years, suffering its own crisis of leadership. The working class accordingly enjoyed a breathing space in which to absorb experience and test its leadership. Its failure to adopt a revolutionary solution to the crisis resulted fundamentally from the degeneration of the Russian Revolution, and not from any effect of the crisis itself. Such a favorable interlude is not likely to be duplicated in the next depression.

The capitalist system, especially in the U.S., has undergone qualitative changes over the past 30 years, changes intimately bound up with the development of monopoly capitalism to a new level. The concentration of economic power in the hands of the giant corporations has proceeded apace and the bourgeoisie has gone much further than in Lenin's time toward developing a consciousness and a *modus operandi* appropriate to this new level of power.

In the days of pre-monopoly "free competition," crises typically appeared as a bolt out of the blue, striking panic into the hearts of the bourgeoisie. They slaughtered capital values at a furious rate as one enterprise after another went under in an intensified struggle of each against all. The only hope of survival for the individual capitalist during a realization crisis was to stay ahead in the competitive struggle, attempting to shift the burden of the crisis onto the workers and other capitalists.

In this way, equilibrium was restored to the system, at the cost of massive unemployment and hunger for the workers, and great losses to the bourgeoisie. Such a pattern was inevitable as long as the market was divided among many producers, none holding a large enough share to exert a dominant influence.

Tendencies in this direction will undoubtedly be observed in the coming crisis, but powerful counter-pressures urge against this course, suggesting action in another direction.

Under monopoly capitalism, a few giants dominate production in each field, and the market no longer appears as a mysterious external force, blowing both good fortune and bad. On the contrary, the size of each capitalist's market-share renders relatively calculable the impact of his own actions on the market as a whole. This permits a degree of manipulation of the market.

Further, in the event of a crisis, the basic contradictions of capitalism, insofar as they affect the profitability of capital, are translatable into immediately visible figures on the corporate balance sheet. Under these circumstances, the big bourgeoisie can be expected to perceive the crisis before it takes its full toll in unemployment and reduced production, and to prepare some measures of self-protection in advance.

Capitalism has become fully aware that the only competition open to it, other than the most well-regulated and "gentlemanly" kind, is full economic warfare—the kind of struggle where somebody *important* is bound to go under and from which the victors emerge with heavy losses. In the next crisis, the capitalist class will most likely act to protect its investments in a much more unified and determined fashion than has been its wont.

Its internal organization is highly improved. A new directing stratum exists—a national power-elite binding together Big Capital, its key representatives in the government, and military bureaucrats into a super-cartel, able to reach speedy consensus on matters of grave importance to the class as a whole without embarrassing public discussion, and then able to implement its decisions by virtue of its access to the pinnacle levers of power.

Changing role of the state

The immense powers of a mammoth state are today being flagrantly exerted on open behalf of monopoly capital. The state's former humble role as a simple guardian of the marketplace pales into nothingness beside its present function as chief underwriter of the great corporations. It not only preserves capitalist property forms, but directly guarantees corporate profits, subordinating all such previous considerations as public opinion and competitive bidding and other superficial legalities of the market.

Even during the long postwar prosperity period, monopoly capitalism depended upon the direct daily intervention of the state to smooth its way. By virtue of governmental arms budgets, monetary manipulations, deficit spending, tax cuts, investment credits, and dozens of other forms of direct and indirect subsidy, all backed up by the huge reservoir of liquid capital made available by mass taxation, the state, in effect, has socialized the process of capital accumulation, including the risks and losses involved therein. Only the profits remain almost wholly private.

During a period of prosperity, the corporate giants are able to shift costs onto other shoulders through more or less concealed operations. In a full realization crisis, they can do so only by means of *direct action against the working class*— wage cuts, speedup, longer hours, anything to wring out the last possible atom of surplus value. Only in this way can production be maintained on some sort of profitable basis.

In the "normal" capitalist crisis, the bourgeoisie obtains some help from the anonymous forces of the market. Unemployment and beggary could be of great value in forcing the proletariat to labor under conditions where both wages and working conditions are cut to the bone. But in his anxiety to protect his investment, each capitalist would greatly prefer that his own workers remain employed; still, he must bow to the market.

Here, as elsewhere, monopoly capitalism has other alternatives. Unemployment, after all, only becomes necessary because of the impossibility of realizing profits on capital under given market conditions and at a given high rate of surplus value. If the rate of surplus value can be forced high enough and quickly enough, the capitalist may continue to realize a profit on his capital, or at least on a greater portion of it, than if he had waited for the wage-rate to fall by "natural" means. To the extent that the monopolistic bourgeoisie are able to work out a program beforehand, they may be able to combine in a united front against the workers to drive down wages and increase the rate of exploitation before calamity arrives.

No realistic program of restabilization in the face of danger can be carried out without the resolute smashing of any capacity of the working class to resist. To this end, it will prove absolutely necessary to subdue and contain *all* independent expressions of opposition—the civil rights movement, the student movement, the general anti-imperialist movements—in order to further circumscribe the role of the labor movement and finally to destroy them all.

At the same time, the drive toward new arenas for profitable investment can only heighten the conflict with the colonial revolution and the workers states. Merely holding back the revolutionary process will no longer do. The bourgeoisie must prove to itself its ability to make the world safe for capitalism once and for all; to this end only a policy of active *counterrevolution* will serve.

The impulsion toward fascism

Capitalism desires two things above all—to realize the highest possible profits on new investments and simultaneously protect the profitability of previous investments. Competitive capitalism was periodically forced to recognize the incompatibility of these two goals, and accept heavy losses. The latest stage of monopoly capitalism, featuring increased control of the market, improved self-organization and all-out government supports, possesses sufficient protective leverage to offer realistic hope to the ruling class that disaster can be avoided.

The *super-state* which is now in construction in all the imperialist centers, for the most part remains cloaked in the forms of bourgeois democracy. In this guise it has probably developed further in the U.S. than elsewhere. However, the super-state can have its full flowering only under fascism.

There is every indication that the present awareness of

the capitalist class is great enough to prompt it to take action at an extremely early stage of crisis. Considerable pressure, for instance, will probably be exerted upon the working class through the medium of the state *before* the appearance of major shutdowns of production.

The class struggle will be intensified by stringent demands made on the workers, and it is improbable that the bourgeois democracy will be able to force significant concessions from them. The bourgeoisie will accordingly be compelled to move toward fascism, perhaps long before the crisis reaches its most profound depths.

But regardless of the bourgeoisie's precise political timetable, its drive to attain more direct political hegemony will require greater political strength than the bourgeoisie unaided can possibly command, and it will certainly demand the intervention of the state before any crisis is far advanced.

Thus, the economic crisis can assume a complex political character from the very outset, which will pose all the fundamental questions of the American Revolution.

The proletarian stage of the Permanent Revolution

The second mainspring of the unparalleled global tension is the proletarian stage of the Permanent Revolution in China, Latin America and Africa.

China

The rapid rise of revolutionary China to the level of a world power and its influence among colonial peoples are promoting new social explosions in Asia, Africa and Latin America.

The Sino-Soviet dispute has occasioned an international public discussion of the problems of proletarian revolution.[8] Not since the early days of the Russian Revolution has a major power propagated the principles of revolution; although the Chinese leadership refuses to identify Stalin with Stalinism, the persistent exposé of the Stalinist doctrine of peaceful coexistence is a source of clarification of principle for all radicals.

Despite grave ideological hangovers from Stalinism and the perseverance of certain bureaucratic practices, the Chinese regime has attacked the problems of building towards socialism in a backward country with keen empirical understanding of the unique economic, political and cultural realities involved. The Chinese Communist Party has presided over a great and continuing revolution that has avoided both the economic pitfalls of Stalinist misrule and the politi-

Leaflet for a Seattle SWP forum in the early 1960s.

cal degeneration accompanying it. International in orientation and increasingly consistent in its Leninist approach to the class struggle, China is, according to our co-thinkers, "the motor force of the colonial revolution."

Cuba

Following the diplomatic break between Cuba and the U.S., the life of the Cuban Revolution hung by a slender thread, threatened daily with annihilation. Now, five years later, the U.S. cannot seriously consider the overthrow of the revolutionary regime save by military conquest; and, while this is the perspective of Wall Street, it cannot be carried out under present circumstances without creating the even greater danger of revolution throughout Latin America. Because of its dramatic accomplishments, the Cuban Revolution constitutes a permanent dagger pointed at the heartland of imperialism.

Just as the Chinese experience spurred and instructed Cuba, the Cuban development in turn has stimulated a higher theoretical and strategic phase of revolutionary politics in Guatemala. With the spread of the colonial revolution, the quality of revolutionary understanding and devotion mounts ever higher; the conscious proletarian internationalism of a guerrilla in Guatemala is both a tribute to the concept and the reality of Permanent Revolution and a deadly threat to imperialism.

Africa

The next big step in the colonial revolution will be the unfolding proletarian revolution in Africa and the consolidation of authentic Pan-Africanism. The bloody repression in the Congo [Zaire] and the upheaval in Algeria result from the tremendous pressures applied by world imperialism in its ruthless attempt to stop the Permanent Revolution from reaching Pan-Africanism.

Imperialism has thus far been able to contain the African

revolution within the framework of capitalism, but it will be unable to maintain this condition once the revolution in South Africa explodes.

The raging civil war in the Congo is to Africa what Guatemala is to Latin America—a crucible in which dynamic answers to continental problems of program and leadership are being forged. The Congo comprises an early stage of preparation in the unfolding Pan-African revolution, which will reach its climax in the Union of South Africa.

In recognition of the new level of the colonial revolution, the U.S. has signified in the Congo, Vietnam and Santo Domingo [the Dominican Republic] that it will use its own military forces for maintaining the status quo rather than depend upon native bourgeois power. This assumption of direct responsibility for further interventions, however, will severely strain U.S. military resources and intensify worldwide resistance to U.S. foreign policy from both allies and enemies.

Decomposition of European reformism

The deterioration of the prospects of European capitalism is symbolized by the plight of the traditional European reformist parties, whose function has been to safely channel the dissatisfaction of the proletariat into patriotic reformism.

Wracked by the power shifts within the Soviet bureaucracy, the Sino-Soviet dispute, the colonial revolution, and pressure from radical workers, the Communist parties in capitalist countries are in chronic crisis. The centrifugal force engendered by their contradictions provides the objective prerequisite for regrouping revolutionary forces on a vaster scale than has been possible since the formation of the Third International.

The Social Democracy, and the British Labour Party in particular, suffers from a similar dilemma of direction, and its internal contradictions pave the way for a workingclass rejection of reformism.

Revolutionary regroupment in the U.S. could be a salient factor in world regroupment, lending vital impetus to the process.

The internationalism of the freedom struggle

The civil rights revolt in the U.S. constantly threatens to paralyze U.S. imperialism at home and abroad. The effect of the Black liberation struggle on the world crisis originates from its internationalist proletarian character. This *character* stamps the Black movement as the *political* means by which the world crisis of capitalism is transmitted to the United States.

European masses identify with the Black skin, because it has become the class symbol of the era—the mark of resistance to oppression. No other American represents the basic condition of the international proletariat; European workers cannot identify with American labor unions because white workers in the U.S. project an image that is devoid of class struggle features.

When Black Americans demonstrate, the masses of the world are invigorated and redouble their efforts to overthrow their yoke, for the Black struggle shows what is best, most vital in the American working class; it even offers hope that the American proletariat, propelled by its most persecuted and conscious sector, will rise en masse to its historic revolutionary mission.

Black people in struggle are relatively immune from Yankee chauvinism, and sense the response to them among the worldwide masses, a response expressed in an anti-imperialist content. Blacks absorb this spirit and re-express it in their own struggle; thus Selma and Saigon become components of the same struggle.

Trotsky once predicted that Afro-Americans would furnish leadership for the African revolution. Apart from the individual prestige and influence of W.E.B. DuBois,[9] this prognosis has not yet materialized, although episodes have occurred showing preliminary signs of such future interrelations. The Montgomery Bus Boycott, for instance, was immediately duplicated in Johannesburg. Today African intellectuals find U.S. Black leadership to be provincial and devoid of social philosophy, but this will be altered when Black leadership which is proletarian and socialist emerges, as it will, in the course of the process of revolutionary regroupment in the U.S.

The basic similarity of social structure in the southern U.S. and South Africa creates an indissoluble tie between Black Americans and Black South Africans. In Africa, the Black proletariat is not burdened with a significant middle- and upper-class of its own and no ground exists upon which reformism may be erected. Neither is there ground for significant reformism in the American South; political realities will not allow it. The new voices of Black proletarian leaders now being heard in the South will travel swiftly overseas as the revolutionary content of the message they carry deepens; the ascending revolution in the U.S. South will indeed breed a leadership capable of sparking emulation in South Africa and providing encouragement and advice on the methods and program of struggle.

The national dilemma

Bonapartism in the state and the growth of fascism

In the period of the death agony of capitalism, fascism is the totalitarian form of rule which the capitalist class resorts to when it can no longer maintain itself through the democratic process.

Fascism may be imposed when capitalism reaches a general crisis and the workers must be made to compensate for employer inability to realize profit on investments. To accomplish it, the capacity of the working class to resist assaults upon its standard of living and its working conditions must be destroyed. This is the task of fascism.

Such a process does not happen overnight, and the capitalist class does not resort to fascism lightmindedly.

As the contradictions of decaying capitalism accumulate, the government first attempts to save itself and its parliamentary institutions by superimposing a dictatorship upon the framework of the bourgeois democracy. Congress and regional legislatures voluntarily surrender their powers on key issues to the central executive authority, which becomes, for a time, a bureaucratic military-police dictatorship: Bonapartism.

Bonapartism, a product of an unstable equilibrium in the class struggle, cannot last because it cannot solve the problems of the capitalist class. The firmer hand of a totalitarian system, plus a devastated working class are required.

Many factors have created the environment for the emergence of Bonapartism in the U.S. today—the Kennedy assassination, the uproar over foreign policy and the spectre of military defeats, the initial steps of the shift toward mass revolutionary action in the South, the explosiveness of the northern ghetto, the necessity for rapid and forceful governmental intervention into the national economy, etc.

Beginning as the protector of law and order after Kennedy's assassination, Lyndon Baines Johnson used his 1964 electoral mandate to take all major policy matters into his own hands. His exercise of exclusive control of foreign affairs and crucial domestic problems, and his individual command of the armed forces and economic manipulation, exemplify the transition to personal rule within the framework of bourgeois democracy.

The willingness of Congress to relinquish its prerogatives and transfer responsibility for all important matters to the executive reflects the deep political crisis rocking U.S. imperialism even before economic contradictions have come to a head.

Johnson and military policy

The proliferation of teach-ins and ideological controversy on Vietnam policy both results from and masks the lack of any legislative or democratic means of changing the policy of the government. LBJ, protector of international imperialism, cannot await congressional deliberation and rationalization before dispatching the arms and troops of counterrevolution. Bypassing a subservient Congress, he manufactures public opinion by going straight to the people via the controlled press and TV.

Johnson and civil rights

The determination of the southern freedom fighters, their deepening ability to rally national and international support, and the proletarian and revolutionary character of their struggle convince the ruling class that it can no longer exclusively entrust the preservation of the southern system to Dixiecrat regimes. Nor can it tolerate the naive illusion of civil rights liberals that the southern system can be reformed without generating gigantic national repercussions.

The Mississippi Freedom Democratic Party has already exposed the incompetence of the southern system in handling its own domestic problems. Beginning as an independent movement that challenged voting restrictions and the white power structure in Mississippi, the MFDP proceeded to challenge the Democratic Party and then Congress itself. The "simple" democratic demand for representation threatens to evolve into an instrument of *dual power* in the South.[10] The national structure of the Democratic Party, i.e., the very foundation of the U.S. political system as established after the Compromise of 1877, is potentially under siege.[11]

Assuming full control on civil rights, LBJ used demagogy and legislative demands to soften the liberals and Black leadership, meanwhile carefully reducing the southern radicals into dependency on the government for protection. He has thus far preserved the southern system.

The willingness of southern congressmen to forego the filibuster during the enactment of two civil rights laws in one year indicates no retreat on their part, but rather underlines the fact that civil rights has long ceased to be a legislative issue. All power to enforce and regulate civil rights rests in the hands of the Texas Bonaparte in the White House.

Johnson and the economy

The Taft-Hartley Act, the Kennedy-Landrum-Griffin Act, anti-communist legislation, etc., have long since guaranteed the subservience of the labor bureaucracy and served to concentrate trade union control in the White House.

All the major factors of economic development depend upon the federal government. The traditional pressure for local economic concessions once exercised by congressmen, previously a dominant activity of Congress, is now a purely secondary function.

Even social welfare measures, once a rallying point for class action, are now left entirely to the president. The liberals and labor bureaucrats gratefully accept LBJ's pennies while conservative congressmen uncharacteristically refrain from any show of opposition.

Control of the class struggle by means of Bonapartism can only be temporary; under conditions of mounting class struggle Bonapartism is the harbinger of fascism. The massive deployment of American troops overseas requires not only public support which liberals can help manufacture, but a crusade-spirit which only a chauvinistic fascist movement can provoke.

In the face of economic stagnation and political crisis, the southern Black struggle and the developing movement in the northern ghetto cannot long be restrained by mere promises. The need to repress an erupting class struggle sharply poses the requirement for fascism, and the foundations for a growing fascist movement are already on hand.

In the 1963 Birmingham protest, the Black militants ultimately inflicted tactical defeat upon the city police and for a few short hours became the masters of the city.[12] This unprecedented manifestation of the grave social crisis of the southern system triggered two simultaneous reflexes in the capitalist class: federal troops were rushed to the scene (after Kennedy's injunction against "extremism on both sides") and the Goldwater boom erupted.

Fascism and Goldwater

Important sections of capital recognized an opportunity to 1) unite the northern ultra-right with the southern reaction on the basis of the white backlash and 2) thereby set the stage for a genuine fascist movement in the U.S.

Objectively, the building of fascism in the U.S. is facilitated by the existence of fascist-like regimes within the political structure. The southern states, essentially based upon the Klan, not only were a model for Hitler, but provide a stable base for fascist growth throughout the U.S. All previous attempts to build a nationwide fascist movement, however, floundered on the difficulty of working out an alliance between the northern ultra-rights and the Klan; the Klans and White Citizen Councils were too consumed by provincialism to be concerned with a national movement. Birmingham shocked them into a cooperative mood.

The ultra-right, meanwhile, steered by the John Birch Society, represents genuine fascist forces; it is a cross-weaving of literally hundreds of anti-communist, racist and fundamentalist Christian groups.[13] Each exhibits, in its own way, one of the cardinal features of fascism: readiness to contain the class struggle and destroy potentially revolutionary forces by extralegal means, and eagerness to create mass combat organs for this purpose.

Born as a terrorist periphery around the government's witch-hunt agencies and committees, the ultra-right grew strong implementing its part of the division of redbaiting labor. Those whom HUAC & Co. could not legally or strenuously prosecute, the ultra-right took care of.[14] Then, they shifted their attack, in typical fascist style, from the communists to the liberals and finally to the government itself. Forced to retreat after the demise of Joe McCarthy, they reemerged onto the political scene towards the end of Eisenhower's reign, when the Cuban Revolution made a shambles of U.S. foreign policy and the Black revolt refused to be deterred by parliamentary maneuverings.

Birmingham and Barry Goldwater supplied the ultra-right with an unequaled opportunity to utilize the apparatus of a major political party for fascist purposes.[15] The entire ultra-right was galvanized into unprecedented activity on behalf of Goldwater in the Republican Party.

Goldwater helped the fascists win a signal victory against Big Capital in the Republican Party. He conformed to their wishes during the campaign, and most significantly, by orienting his program toward the southern and northern racists, he succeeded in acquiring at least a temporary alliance with the most reactionary southern regimes. As the centralizing force for the entire ultra-right, he thus laid the basis for close national collaboration among the fascist forces.

The Goldwater campaign was by no means a full-blown fascist campaign, but it admirably served the needs of U.S. fascism at the moment. Its object was not to win the election, but to cement alliance with the Klan and sow mistrust of the democratic process, and it succeeded.

Perhaps Goldwater has no greater personal ambition than to have his own TV program. He obviously is no ideal Fuehrer. Nevertheless, he was eminently adequate for the 1964 phase of fascist growth. He may be superseded as the movement develops, but it would be a serious error of political analysis to mistake his advocacy of laissez-faire capitalism for inane outmoded conservatism. His nostalgia for the past is *absolutely typical fascist demagoguery*.

The capitalist class in general was not prepared to call in

the fascists to assume mastery of the house of government, nor were the fascists prepared to take over this role. Had Goldwater won the election, it would have been a setback for them; they would have found themselves precipitated into the midst of a huge welfare state that they are committed to destroy, and they were not yet prepared with the means of destruction. Forced to live with the welfare state, they would have had to temporize with it and become dangerously absorbed by it.

The capitalist class used the Goldwater campaign to whip the Democrats and speed up the Bonapartist trend. Johnson, the Democratic Party and the Republicans in Congress are striving mightily to demonstrate that they can govern the country by means of a modification of bourgeois democracy in the direction of increased centralization, and thereby protect capital adequately. To them, the lesson of Goldwaterism is that the moment they falter in dealing with present or future crises, they will be cast aside by Big Business and replaced with the totalitarian state.

The U.S., then, does not stand on the brink of fascism; the present form of the coalescence of fascist groupings is an elementary stage of development. Still, it would be highly unfortunate if the Socialist Workers Party shortly found itself marching to the concentration camps with signs reading "this is not classical fascism."[16]

The crisis of capitalist democracy is very real. The colonial revolutions abroad and the Black revolt at home shake up the equilibrium at the center of world imperialism. As the general crisis of capitalism matures, it will become increasingly apparent that Goldwaterism in 1964 was an important milestone in the development of American fascism.

The fascists know that in the final analysis, greater forces than those presently mobilized will be needed to stop the onrushing Black struggle. They know that the basic social changes required to satisfy the Black people's elementary demands can be achieved only by a social revolution. They are geared to stop this focal point of the domestic and world crisis—the Black movement—as decisively as they can.

Revolution in the South

Uneven and combined development in the U.S.

The emerging revolution in the South, initiated by the Black people, is an expression of the uncompleted tasks of the bourgeois revolution. But the southern social system has become so intertwined with the basic socio-economic structure of U.S. capitalism that even though the present stage of the Black movement has forced concessions from the federal government, has compelled the Bourbons to retreat, and is steadily gaining ground, no qualitative change has been effected in the southern police states. Furthermore, Big Capital recognizes that any substantial change in the South would disrupt the entire politico-economic equilibrium of American capitalism.

The northern ghetto, responsive to the incipient southern revolution but propelled into action by its own contradictions, breaks out in sharpening clashes with the power structure. The entrenched nature of northern ghetto conditions becomes more obvious every day to the community; there clearly is no cure for racial discrimination under the status quo.

There is no necessary conflict between the northern and southern movements; they are complementary parts of a single nationwide movement for liberation. This unified character is expressed in a constant North-South intermigration, which is an important vehicle for the interpenetration of experiences and ideas of Black militants everywhere. Apparent differences of aims and interests are a product of the profound crisis of leadership and not of differing objectives. The inherent drive of the entire Black proletariat is for a new society that can encompass basic changes in the economic, social, political and cultural foundations of this society.

For 15 years, the incipiently revolutionary Black movement has been frustrated by its middleclass reformist leadership, but a new leadership representing the Black proletariat is emerging. Robert Williams was a forerunner of this trend. From Harlem, Detroit, Mississippi, Texas and hundreds of localities, the new leadership is starting to come forth. James Boggs, Bill Epton, Fanny Lou Hamer, Victoria Gray and the many others, now express key aspects of the profound revolutionary spirit pervading the Black working class.[17]

The most acute manifestation of the uneven political development in the American working class is the existence of a tangible and concrete pre-revolutionary situation in the southern states, while in the North, the pre-revolutionary situation which will unfold in due order does not at present exist.

This unevenness imposes extraordinary burdens upon the leadership of the southern movement and even greater responsibilities upon the revolutionary party in the U.S.

We can confidently expect that the revolutionary spirit generated in the South will radiate in all directions and that the general crisis of capitalism will eventually propel the northern working class into political mobility. However, the southern revolution cannot wait for a general crisis of capitalism; it is following laws of development that grow out of the sociology of the South.

The basic strategic problem is this: the southern revolution, with the forces it will be able to mobilize in the South, could realistically expect to win against the southern police-state. However, its leaders must anticipate that when victory appears imminent, the capitalist class will require the government to intervene with "whatever force is necessary" to preserve the status quo and stop the "Communist aggression" as defined by the "Johnson-Monroe" Doctrine.[18]

In spite of the fact that a revolutionary situation in the North may not have matured by this decisive moment, it

Seattle SWP takes part in a 1963 protest of an anti-communist rally organized by two notorious segregationists, former Army Major General Edwin Walker and Billy James Hargis. (Photo by Vince Davis)

will be mandatory for us to be able to call forth a sympathetic movement of sufficient magnitude to prevent the government from carrying out the demands placed on it by the capitalist class; otherwise, the southern revolution will be drowned in blood.

This conjuncture must be elaborately prepared in word and deed by going to the mass movements now with the message of the southern revolution. The main responsibility for this alerting action rests with the conscious revolutionary vanguard. Implementing this strategy of revolutionary defense will constitute one of the main bridges between the Black movement and the working class as a whole, and, in a companion development, the living link between the socialist movement and both.

Present conjuncture of the southern movement

The crisis of leadership has deepened during the past two years.

In 1956, the essentially conservative Dr. Martin Luther King, Jr. represented a militant wing of the civil rights movement. The power of the upsurge of the Black masses during the past few years can be gauged by the fact that although it pushed the King leadership leftward, the Southern Christian Leadership Conference (SCLC) is today the right wing of the southern movement, and its leadership is tolerated only because the revolutionary spirit of most Student Non-Violent Coordinating Committee (SNCC) and Mississippi Freedom Democratic Party (MFDP) militants has not yet crystallized into a definite program.

The crisis of leadership derives from the fact that nobody presents a convincing answer to the basic problem: *How can you win in the South?*

The official view of all the leadership groups in the southern movement is that the federal government must step in and install democratic rights; this is the goal of the movement. But the government evinces no such inclination, using its power essentially to maintain the status quo while it issues demagogic promises.

The basic distinction between the SCLC, Congress of Racial Equality (CORE) and SNCC lies only in the degree of mass action each advocates to pressure the government to act decisively.

Caught between the maneuverism and opportunism of the northern liberals who help support the movement, and the authentic revolutionary spirit emanating from the Delta, SNCC officers are in a constant quandary. They vacillate between militant anti-capitalist speeches and demonstrations, and compromises or silence when the unbearable tension between them and King's outright reformism demands a resolution.

They have discovered a unique method of bureaucratic

control—utter administrative confusion buttressed by a doctrine of absolute activism—which provides no formal channels for policy debates leading to decisions. Their unanimity rule virtually precludes development by experience. As a result, the SNCC staff of active field secretaries and other militants is in a chronic and unbelievably bitter policy crisis.

The crisis *of* leadership has grown over into a crisis *in* the leadership. The internal convulsions are bound to produce a leap into an outright revolutionary orientation if a large enough section of SNCC clearly understands this fact. The fulfillment of the promise of the Reconstruction[19] and the destruction of the police state in the South will not be achieved except by revolution, *the fire and the sword.*

Hundreds, perhaps thousands, of southern Black workers already know and understand the implications of this fact. They comprise a substantial wing of the Mississippi Freedom Democratic Party.[20] They are in the process of producing a new kind of leadership oriented to break the programmatic logjam of the reformists and solve the crisis of leadership in the South. Thereby, they are laying the basis for ending the leadership crisis in the North as well.

Mississippi Freedom Democratic Party

The MFDP is the most momentous political development of our time in this country. It is currently stirring up much consternation in government and civil rights circles. Its challenge to the seating of the Mississippi congressmen expresses its basic boldness and energy.

It is a genuine mass movement of Black workers and sharecroppers of Mississippi. Existing for two years in the deepest South, it shows great capacity for survival and development. No other political formation of this type has been able to establish itself in the South since Populism was crushed at the turn of the century.[21]

The leadership core of the MFDP is determined, outspoken, independent and radical; its objective is to take political power away from the Democratic Party of Mississippi. Although it has sought to utilize the national Democratic Party as both a sounding board for its political demands and a source of public support, the indigenous Mississippi leadership is quite aware of the character of the Democratic Party and considers its ephemeral alliance with northern Democrats to be a temporary tactic. But the confusion created by this tactic is deepened by the liberals and the Communist Party who use it as a gimmick to pressure northern radicals and Black militants into continued support of the Democrats.

The clash of the tactic with principle is becoming abundantly clear. The Administration has proven itself to be a most effective enemy, and the impotent, hypocritical liberals are exposed as down-the-line Johnsonites. As the MFDP extends into other states, which it must do, the leadership will have to determine if each local movement must enact the charade of pretending to be good Johnson Democrats, when repetition of the masquerade will clearly demoralize and slow down the tempo of the movement.

Real independence means a definite break with the Democratic Party, and continued growth of the MFDP requires that it assume a structural identity of its own. The leaders are capable of such a break; they broke more intimate ties with the Mississippi Black clergy and middle class when they realized that these ties were a fetter on the movement.

The MFDP will survive by extending the movement throughout the South and formalizing its objectively independent nature and program. It sorely needs a transitional program to provide a political foundation for breaking with the Democratic Party. (See Appendix One, "A Transitional Program for the Southern Revolution.")

Revolt in the ghetto

In the South, democratic demands are the motive force of the revolution. As happened in Cuba, the ultimate demands of the democratic revolution become the transitional demands of the proletarian revolution. But the North faces a more complicated problem; nothing short of socialism offers any meaningful solution for the ghetto, and different slogans and tactics are needed.

Attempts to ameliorate the desperate conditions of daily life through rent strikes, struggles against police brutality, the fight for jobs and better schools, etc., are primarily significant as stages of the process toward socialist political action, for such reforms or mobilizations, of themselves, cannot liberate the ghetto. Unless they are tied to prospects for a fundamental social change, they breed demoralization and cynicism.

A conscious vanguard in the ghetto would tie itself closely to the southern movement. It would express directly what southern spokesmen may have to say obliquely, thoroughly exposing the machinations of the Democratic Party, popularizing the program of the "Constitutional" revolution in the South, and mobilizing support and training cadres for it. Simultaneously, such a northern leadership would organize socialist political action.

Lincoln likened slavery to a prison cell, sealed by a lock with seven interdependent keys, "...and these keys...distributed to the far corners of the earth." A revolutionary program unifying the Black movement North and South is the master key to this lock. Many have searched for it, but few with the talents of Malcolm X.

Malcolm X

The story of Malcolm X is the saga of a man growing politically and intellectually before our eyes—a process that the reactionaries had to stop. The murder of Malcolm was a blow to the Black and socialist movements, and it thrust into the forefront the complex question of the character of the Black Muslims.

The 1963 SWP resolution on the Black movement

states: "The Muslims, headed by Elijah Muhammad, are the most dynamic tendency in the northern Negro community today."[22] All the Muslim sympathizers, the SWP included, have studiously avoided the question of exactly who killed Malcolm.

Malcolm knew that Mr. Muhammad's goon squad would murder him, and he widely publicized this apprehension, yet the *Militant* adopted the platitudinous position that he was "killed by capitalism." Well, so was Frank Little, so was Medgar Evers, and so, in the final analysis, was Leon Trotsky, whose murderers in the Kremlin were a product of capitalism's pressure on the Soviet Union.[23] It is obvious that Malcolm's break with the Muslims, his trip to Africa and the Middle East, and his pledge to return to the South all constituted good reason for the white capitalist reaction to do away with him. But in all such cases of political murder, it is essential, and in the socialist tradition, to *identify the specific source and analyze the motives involved.* Otherwise, the victim dies in vain, the loss is absolute instead of relative, and nobody learns anything from the tragedy.

The dilemma of the SWP is that any analysis of the Muslims would reveal the serious basic error of the 1963 convention line. The inability to distinguish between a reactionary and a progressive social formation has placed the party in an embarrassing position, as one by one the ingrained separatist movements reveal themselves to be extremely rightwing, while those who have progressed past separatism are starting to become dynamic contenders for leadership in the Black community.

Supposed friends of the SWP turn out to be Goldwaterites. The Indemnity Movement, a peripheral Muslim organization, shows little interest in indemnity and much concern with *The Protocols of Zion,* how the Jews control the Black press and keep Black actors out of motion pictures, and similar dynamic topics.[24] The Bay Area Afro-Americans are found to have close ties with the John Birch

Society and conduct joint West Coast tours with them. Rev. Cleage deserts.[25] The Black Muslims are shown to have working relations not only with cops but with the Klan.

An objective analysis of the Muslims reveals that they possess all the qualifications (enumerated by Trotsky and other Marxist authorities) of a fascist movement: middle-class leadership grouped around a messiah, declassed social base, social demagoguery, ties with capital, exploitation of religious mysticism, anti-Semitism, subordination of women, race fetishism, and trained strong-arm squadrons.

These squads have never been used against the oppressor because they are oriented in a different direction— against rebels. Beginning as a disciplinary force against recalcitrant members of the sect, then extending jurisdiction to the ghetto at large, they become an extralegal political police force in the ghetto—and they are the assassins of Malcolm X.

The Muslims alone bear the responsibility for his murder, for it was perpetrated in the service of Muslim principle, policy and necessity, regardless of whether CIA or FBI agents were involved. The latter always stand ready to cooperate in the frame-up and/or murder of a militant.

Finally, the Black Muslims, in addition to everything else, betray a typically American feature: the top "prophets" are operating a hugely successful racket.

The white fascist movement knows that it cannot subdue the ghetto alone; it would be cut to pieces. It desperately needs as an ally, at least in the first bloodletting stages, an independent Black separatist organization. It has to gain a point of support in the ghetto, support which many separatist organizations, including the Muslims, stand ready to offer in return for hegemony over the ghetto and economic partnership in the economic exploitation of the Black consumer-goods market.

If fascism should succeed in the United States, the pattern of its relation with the ghetto would be generally as follows: the ghetto will be terrorized by a well-organized Black ally of the white fascists. After the socialists, communists, integrationists, labor unionists and liberals have been eliminated, the ghetto will be safe for takeover by white fascist gangs who will then proceed to annihilate their erstwhile allies, the Muslims, or other separatists. The entire ghetto then becomes transformed into a gigantic gas chamber.

Malcolm was a defector who had to *break* with the Muslims in order to be free to start to lead his followers *into* the living struggle and free to start the difficult process of developing towards political radicalism and revolutionary internationalism.[26] *The Muslims had to split.* What was viable and militant about them could not be contained within the rigid structural framework of a utopian and petty-bourgeois monolith.

Malcolm was killed precisely *because* he split. An honest man, probing for answers, he finally began to expose the demagoguery and sinister connections of the Muslims. He was tearing them apart and that is why he was murdered. And that is why the SWP cannot say why he was murdered.

It is highly unfortunate that the SWP, eager to welcome what it hoped was the long-awaited Black nationalist-separatist movement, renounced all its scientific criteria of evaluation and treated the Black Muslims with a respect bordering on adulation. Every dangerous, reactionary, and ignorant prejudice of the Muslims was justified—rationalized away on the grounds that an oppressed minority has the right to these notions as a result of its special experience, as if the starving, demoralized and desperate masses of German unemployed had no "cause" for their eager latching on to Nazi-dom.

Muslims will someday "change" and "grow," we were assured. Even today, representatives of the party of Leon Trotsky in the U.S. condone Muhammad's alliance with the American Nazi Party and the Klan as justified by his right of "self-determination." It is devoutly to be hoped that the paternalism which views Black people on the wrong side of the barricades as dynamically progressive will someday "change" and "grow."

It is necessary to state once again: The Black Muslims are a reactionary religious organization with a conservatizing and terrorizing effect on the community. If Malcolm's whole life and death proved nothing more, they exposed the nature of the Muslims. Malcolm's self-confessed "zombie" days of Black Muslim orthodoxy, his awakening and defection, and his evolution toward socialism all reveal the significant peculiarities of the Muslim movement, as well as the differences and similarities between the Muslims and European fascist movements.

1) Although both Fascisti and Nazis attracted serious rebel types from the plebeian masses who developed opposition to the middleclass leadership, this friction did not produce important convulsions until *after* the fascists took power. The Muslims, however, operate among proletarians of a super-oppressed minority group, which made it impossible for Malcolm to long resist the magnetism of the proletarian cause.

2) During the past few years, the Muslims enjoyed a heyday out of all proportion to their objective attractive power. They essentially fed upon a 40-year default of the socialist and communist movements—their failure to provide a revolutionary program upon which the Black movement could erect a militant leadership. The consequent vacuum propelled a far better quality of rebels toward the Muslims than was their due.

3) The provocative Muslim demagogy even fooled some radicals who had never actually read Hitler's harangues for comparison, nor digested Trotsky and Guérin.[27] Instead of helping the Muslims' captives to escape, these radicals locked the door on them.

It is equally necessary to state once again that nationalism, for Black radicals and sophisticates, is a transitory and transitional form of recoil from the middleclass, reformist and legalistic integrationist leaders of the M.L. King-Roy Wilkins variety.[28] The flirtation of these nationalists with separatism can only be short-lived as the separatists expose their reactionary course. In life, the content of northern "nationalism" and southern "integrationism" are identical—towards revolution and towards an integrated society in the U.S.[29]

Freedom Now Party

In a bold and serious attempt to solve the crisis of leadership in the North by building a new Black vanguard, William Worthy launched the Freedom Now Party (FNP).[30]

He conceived it as a militant, radical and transitional political formation which would break the Muslims' sectarian stranglehold on Harlem and direct the "nationalist" anti-white bitterness towards political defiance of the capitalist state apparatus. Worthy knew that only radical politics, i.e., going to the roots of the problem, could combat the growing forces of terrorism and Muslim abstentionism. He sought a bridge to radical internationalism, starting at the mood of the moment—race solidarity and independence—and spanning the gap to socialist class consciousness.

But this party, saddled with the nebulous and basically reformist program imposed upon it by the SWP, was doomed to failure. Instead of an anti-capitalist program and a truly dynamic new cadre, FNP got hung up on the fetish that "Black is Enough." *All Black!* was trumpeted with the élan of "The Marseillaise,"[31] and most Black proletarian radicals were bewildered.

The conception that Black, alone, and by its very nature, must be progressive, betrays inroads of mysticism into a party founded on materialism.

Further, this view is in diametric opposition to everything that Trotsky ever wrote, particularly his view of the Permanent Revolution. In reference to especially oppressed "peoples," Trotsky expounded the Bolshevik (as opposed to Menshevik) position that the *proletariat* is the only *class* capable of leadership; therefore, he said, in the building of political parties among especially oppressed sectors, *the proletariat has to maintain its independence.*

But in the Freedom Now Party, the Black proletariat was virtually invited to get lost. For in the official SWP view, the Black community is without class differentiation and conflict; everything is just Black, a homogeneous mass requiring only "unity" to solve U.S. race relations. SWP's Freedom Now propaganda was engineered not to stimulate growth of a revolutionary proletarian leadership, but to achieve a magical All-Black Unity.

Black unity, however, can be achieved only on the basis of the united front for specific demands. To try to carry it further at this time, into the realm of a permanent political party, is fuzzy people's frontism.[32] There are class divisions and conflicts in the Black community; while they are rarely identical to the basic worker-boss confrontation in general capitalist society, they are so qualitatively real that Black workers cannot and usually will not subordinate themselves to either the tiny Black bourgeoisie or the growing petty-bourgeoisie. Yet this subordination was implicit in the All-Black Unity Party slogan.

The SWP majority proclaims that it alone fully appreciates the independent aspect of the race question; indeed, it has transformed the independence of the movement, labeled as an "*aspect*" by the 1948 resolution on the Black movement, into the basic *nature* of the question. Yet the Freedom Now Party experience illustrates once more again how the SWP completely discounts the specific laws of motion of the Black struggle and subordinates them to the laws of trade union development.

The race question (like everything else) is reshaped by the SWP to fit into labor movement criteria. The All-Black Unity Party slogan is conceived in terms of the *labor party*

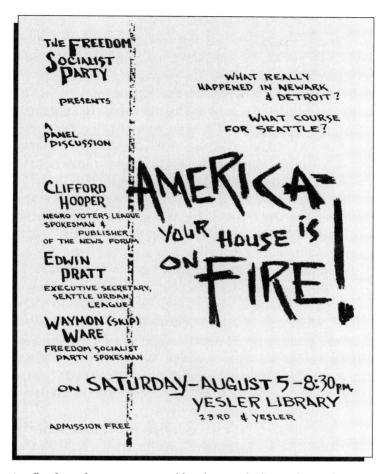

Leaflet for a forum sponsored by the newly formed Freedom Socialist Party on the 1967 Newark and Detroit riots. Panelists included civil rights leader Edwin Pratt, who in 1969 was shot to death by an unknown political assassin.

slogan, wherein *program is not decisive* because independent workingclass political organization *by itself* is progressive and leads to radical programmatic conclusions. All-Black political action appears to the SWP leadership to be the same thing. But it is not. Program, not race, is the decisive determinant here, because *race by itself has no political character.*

When "All-Black" becomes a *program*, no orientation to class struggle politics is possibly forthcoming, because All-Black derives from the theory of Black Self-Determination—a theory that pivots around the central point of the right of Blacks to secede from the American proletariat.

The effect of nationalist theory, then, upon an organization originally capable of orienting towards the Black vanguard of the *working class*, was that same curious amalgam of reformism and laborism that has characterized most SWP theory and tactics in regard to the Black struggle.

The Freedom Now Party was paralyzed by the spectre of "Self-Determination" hovering over it. It ended up catering to disoriented layers of the Black population, and instead of raising political understanding to a higher level, it congealed a dead-end anti-white ideology. The crisis of Black leadership was not helped by FNP; on the contrary, it was rendered more acute. Designated as transitional to Marxism, it actually encouraged a transition to much different quarters. Because it was reformist and lacking class character, it was sociologically nowhere and had to seek a home. It became a transition to everything except the SWP—to the Muslims, Progressive Labor Party, capitalist coalition politics or withdrawal from the struggle.

Unless the demon of separatism is finally exorcised, the SWP itself will not be able to structurally assimilate more than one-percent of the Blacks who join it. It is not surprising that Black worker members become demoralized and repelled by the tactic of subordination to the Black middle class, as it materialized, for example, in Detroit, where the party leadership engineered a bloc with Rev. Cleage around the minimum program of All-Black. While superior to the reformist integrationists, Cleage is likewise a conservative and a reformist, and is genuinely antilabor as well; the limitations of the Black middle class are clearly stamped upon him. A group of militants opposed him, demanding a more advanced program for FNP. The unprincipled character of the 1963 convention line took form in the choice made by the SWP leadership to form an alliance with a conservative antilabor petty-bourgeois instead of with these militant workers. The latter feel there is no workingclass solidarity in the SWP, and in this instance they are right.

The emancipation of women

The defiance of one woman, Rosa Parks, sparked the Montgomery Bus Boycott and inaugurated a new era in American politics.[33] It was no accident that a Black woman worker played this role. Two hundred years of history and two revolutions conditioned and tempered her for leadership of the Third American Revolution. The mass movement for civil rights in Mississippi is becoming more consciously revolutionary every day, and the leaders of this movement are predominately women.[34]

They have the support of an important section of southern white women, even though this support is characteristically quiet and even secret. For many decades, hundreds of southern white women have worked clandestinely on the "Problem" in the crevices of the police state, and on behalf of their Black sisters in bondage.[35] They had come to realize the unmentionable fact that southern white males were the lordly beneficiaries of a two-edged oppression: they robbed the Black woman of any acknowledged paternity for her child, and they hypocritically degraded the white woman into a truly segregated, dependent, chattel status. The myth of "sacred" white womanhood is one of the focal points of the ideology of white supremacy and ties the struggle for the emancipation of women directly to the Black liberation struggle.

This heritage of the economics of color slavery was restored to the South after the Ku Klux Klan destroyed the Reconstruction and established the police state, sharecropping and the chivalric code to insure segregation. But the revival of female lineage in the Black community ironically conferred a real benefit upon the Black woman, for the matriarchal conditions that emerged molded her into a figure of independence, self-reliance, responsibility and resourcefulness. Always engaged in social production, she was integral to the economy, to the community and to the family.

Accordingly, as a worker, a Black person, and a woman, she represented the three strands of American repressive culture; every prejudice focused on her and she felt deeply the threefold nature of the fight for freedom. She was destined objectively for her function today as the vanguard of political consciousness, spirit and vitality; in Mississippi she runs for Congress, organizes farm labor unions and schools, confronts—and confounds—the Black men of her own movement with her initiative and firm resistance to all their attempts to subordinate and subdue her. For every Gloria Richardson who retires into domesticity, scores of Black women leaders are becoming professionals for the movement.[36]

They face thorny problems. Indeed, they face a double problem, for the nature of both the "race question" and the "woman question" is analogous. Each has a *dual* nature: exploitation on the job connects them each to the class struggle, while generalized political, legal and cultural oppression against them as a special "inferior" group confer an *independent* character to their struggle.

All dark-skinned people are victims of color prejudice. Similarly, what Lenin called "an entire sex," regardless of class distinction and regardless of whether they are wage-earners, is the victim of social prejudice. Women's "inferiority" derives from the condition of the *majority* of women, who are excluded by economics and tradition from participating in public social production and are confined to private domestic labor, leading lives of personal service to isolated families.

A man engages in social production, and thereby serves society; a woman essentially serves her man. Since the majority of women are peripheral to public industry and objectively dependent, all women are stereotyped as secondary. All come to represent an undifferentiated domestic function as a sex.

While the ruling class imposes a generally parasitic existence upon its wives, the wives and families of the working man are absolutely essential to the preservation of the capitalist system. The wife delivers and nurtures children, the future labor power of society, and her labor helps reproduce the daily labor power of her husband; yet both these functions are carried out with the smallest possible cost to the capitalist, who has providently arranged for the worker to bear economic responsibility for his family. A wife assures his domestic needs in the cheapest manner. Accordingly, the family as the economic unit of society constitutes a permanent source of proletarian conservatism and the basis for capitalist super-exploitation. Lord Delaware, requesting women for the American colonies, happily looked forward to "honest laborers burthened with children."

Wage slavery is the basic means of exploitation under capitalism, but it is also the foundation of "equality" in this society. In a market economy, human equality is established through the exchange of commodities by their owners, and however depressed the wages and conditions of the proletarian, he still appears in the marketplace as the owner and seller of that most precious of all commodities—labor-power. Through ownership of this commodity and through its exchange for wages, the mark of socially necessary human labor-power under capitalism, he not only asserts his social relationship and equality with others, he also establishes his political and economic strength—his ability to bargain and change the conditions of his life.

The housewife, however, does not appear in the marketplace as a seller of commodities, and however necessary her domestic labor may be to the maintenance of the family, she does not *sell* her labor power. In a society whose distinctive feature is the social character of labor and the wage system, the labor of women is private, personal and unpaid—hence, *slave labor*. Where a man sells his labor-power for a limited time, the wife sells *all* of herself to him. The formerly social and public productive labor of women has been reduced by bourgeois monogamy to the degrada-tion of slave labor, dignified only by its modern-dress label —Occupation Housewife. Housework is simply secondary to "the acquisition of the necessities of life by the man; the latter was everything, the former an unimportant extra."[37]

But man is fundamentally a producing and a creative animal; dependency and parasitism, even more than sla-very, are degenerative to the mind and body. The rebellion against this condition therefore transcends all classes of society.

> While upon the woman of the working class the cross of capitalist society rests heaviest in all ways, not one of her sisters in all the upper ranks but bears some share of the burden, or, to be plainer, of the smudge—and what is more to the point, they are aware of it. Accordingly, the invocation of the "Rights of Woman" not only rouses the spirit of the heaviest sufferers under capitalist soci-ety, and thereby adds swing to the blows of the male militants in their efforts to overthrow the existing order, it also lames the adversary by raising sympathizers in his own camp, and inciting sedition among his own retinue.
>
> –Daniel DeLeon,
> Preface to *Woman Under Socialism*[38]

Moreover, the capitalist system itself creates the condi-tions for the emancipation of women.

> However terrible and disgusting the dissolution, under the capitalist system, of the old family ties may appear, nevertheless, modern industry, by assigning as it does

an important part in the process of production, outside the domestic sphere, to women, to young persons, and to children of both sexes, creates a new economic foundation for a higher form of the family and the relations between the sexes.

–Karl Marx, *Capital*[39]

It is therefore "plain," writes Engels, "that the first condition for the liberation of the wife is to bring the whole female sex back into public industry." However, the modern family is still "founded on the open or concealed domestic slavery of the wife" and within the family, the man "is the bourgeois and the wife represents the proletariat."[40] The process of achieving "higher" relations is made demonstrably tortuous by the psychology of superiority induced in men as a concomitant of their privileged "bourgeois" status.

The Black movement for emancipation, like the labor movement before it, is running up against obstacles imposed by these ancient prejudices. The doctrine and practice of male supremacy has a long history of corrosive effect on the solidarity, momentum and morale of the movement.

The masculine mystique

Racial emancipation often becomes associated with a fetish of male supremacy—"Be a *Man!*" The secondary role played by Black men for so long in society, the economy and the family is frequently over-compensated for as they press for civil rights.

Women are an available outlet for their self-assertion, and there ensues either a paterfamilias despotism, as endorsed by the Muslims, or a more subtle and sophisticated assumption of male supremacy derived from campus sociology, orthodox Freudianism, and general practice. The male leadership is frequently insensitive to the drive of Black women for acknowledged equality within the movement, for their right to do the work they are qualified and ready to do.

An added complication ensues when the intersection of chronic male chauvinism with the relatively advanced interraciality of the movement leads to the Black women identifying the chauvinism of the men with the relatively advanced sexual code characteristic of many of the young white women working in SNCC (Student Non-Violent Coordinating Committee). The frank rejection of middleclass puritanism by these northern women represents a partial break with the feminine mystique. They want to live as entire human beings, on all levels of life, acting directly on society as men do. Yet they are not prepared to contend for equality with men, for such a stance means a fight. Like most U.S. women, they are conditioned to be "feminine," i.e., softer and nobler creatures by virtue of their noncompetitiveness. The potentially disastrous corollary of this submissiveness is their indisposition to support the Black women who are contending and competing because their leadership role is jeopardized by the regressive ideology of the men. The Black women find themselves isolated and defensively tend to adopt an objectively retrogressive moral code which deepens the gulf between the women still further.

The solution lies in the very process of working together, which offers promise of their ultimate convergence and alliance on the basis of their mutual oppression by men and by society. In order to endure and develop, the Black liberation movement, North and South, is going to have to rise to heights unachieved by any existing labor or political organization: it is going to have to *come to grips with the woman question.*

White women will have to develop consciousness and militancy on this question, and learn to bolster the course of Black women towards equality and leadership. Black women will have to see through the hypocrisy of the white middleclass norms of family stability and propriety. Black and white men will have to learn to subordinate subjective prejudices to a program and practice that incorporates appreciation of the woman question as an objective social issue that cannot be separated from civil rights. Equality and emancipation are indivisible.

The woman question will then be elevated from the back room into a proudly raised public issue of the liberation movement. Black and white women, exerting their strength through solidarity, will soon persuade Black and white men to cease and desist from the habits and outlook of the slaveholder, and the movement will soar to new levels.

The murkiness of the subject of women's oppression is due to unconsciousness or denial of it among the majority of women. But as women begin to move in instinctive defense of civil rights, they will discern the similarity between the two struggles; the Black struggle becomes the training ground for the movement of women's emancipation, and each strengthens the other.

The overpowering social and cultural influence of the southern system upon the rest of the country has produced a twin oppression in every walk of life: race and sex discrimination go hand in hand, and one cannot survive without the other.

Concomitantly, the militancy of an ideologically emancipated woman can have far-reaching effects in any sphere where she finds herself; this is particularly true in the labor movement.

Women and labor

The isolated home cannot possibly organize the woman at the point of her production; instead, it disorganizes and alienates her. Entry into public production transfers her from outer space into a socialized arena of struggle for both the class and her sex.

The logic of feminism is to expand inexorably into generalized radicalism, and women become doubly mistrusted and disliked by the labor bureaucracy, which prefers to leave workers unorganized and wages unequalized rather than absorb new women militants into the union and into the leadership. The woman question runs like a red thread through the problems of organizing the unorganized, industrial unionism in the North and South, the gap between skilled and unskilled labor, unemployment and marginal employment, and the determination of union policy, especially in strikes. (The movie *Salt of the Earth* vividly depicted the *decisive* importance of respecting and utilizing the advanced militancy of women.)[41]

As the ratio of blue to white-collar workers continues its reversal, women workers are becoming predominantly white-collar, and the labor force of key industries is becoming increasingly white-collar. Yet because these new jobs are filled mostly by women, they remain outside union jurisdiction, and the organized sections of American labor dwindle. The current impasse of the telephone union, among others, is a result of the tradition of second-class economic and leadership status for women even when they form the *bulk* of the ranks. This paternalism is duplicated in virtually every existing union—garment, auto and aircraft, printing trades, electric, laundry clerks, building service, etc. Even waitresses and stenographers are usually represented by male officials.

To make matters worse, the failure of the labor movement to recognize the special problems and talents of the woman worker, to build a woman leadership, and to overcome its historic drag in this field, tends to be more or less duplicated in the mass movements of the present day, jeopardizing their future, as illustrated in the civil rights organizations. But as Black insurgency in the South intensifies militancy in the northern civil rights and labor movements, the advanced nature of the drive for sex equality in Mississippi and Alabama will spread to the women in the labor movement and in political organizations elsewhere, spurring them to greater efforts and their organizations to higher development.

The intimate connection between the woman question and the future of American labor—a connection today provided not only through women in industry but through women in the Black struggle—must not be underestimated.

The labor movement

A fundamental source of the culturally inherited conservatism of American white workers is their race prejudice. Closely allied to white supremacy, the doctrine and practice of male superiority is another mark of the backwardness of the class.

The white-supremacy fixation of many workers creates an irrational bond between worker and boss, and shatters the real bond between workers. The inability of the organized proletariat to build a class political party of its own is, in large measure, traceable to white racism. Accepting the policy of a labor federation or congress that includes Jim Crow locals,[42] or that retreats from an organizing drive because it cannot and will not resist the barrier of racism, would be inconceivable to a *class-conscious* worker. The failure of "Operation Dixie" to extend unionism into the South accordingly sealed off the unions from further expansion, froze them into instruments of the white aristocracy of labor, paralyzed them before the onslaught of reaction emanating from the South, and rendered them defenseless against the open shop.[43]

The feminine mystique, so prominent in the labor movement, remains, along with racism, a significant factor in union degeneration. The super-exploitation of Black labor was challenged by the Congress of Industrial Organizations (CIO) 30 years ago. That women are a historically older, and often even more exploited, reservoir of cheap labor, is still regarded as "natural" by the bulk of trade unionists.

The basic unevenness of American political development is illustrated by the situation wherein revolutionary Black people are driving forward while the privileged, conservative and apathetic union movement lies dormant, its bureaucracy incorporated into the state apparatus and its locals serving as adjuncts of the Democratic Party. Truly, trade unions are drawing close to and growing together with the capitalist state machinery. U.S. unions have traveled a long way down that road of degeneration foreseen by Trotsky in 1940.

In the '30s, the CIO virtually transformed the organized labor movement from craft to industrial unionism. The dynamic virility of the movement contained classic revolutionary implications, promising first an advance toward a labor party. The extended war boom, however, combined with relentless government harassment, reversed this trend to such an extent that the present union bureaucracy once again represents only privileged sectors of the working class. Even in the mass production industries, union control is largely in the hands of skilled and high-seniority workers who, in accordance with their own narrow outlook, operate at the expense of the lower-paid production workers.

Since the Wagner Act, the CIO had come to depend on government intervention in order to extend the union movement.[44] National Labor Relations Board mediation and assistance were the CIO's levers of growth. The Taft-Hartley Act, however, so narrowed the scope of NLRB aid that the expansion of unionism was virtually ended and its very existence lay at the mercy of the government. This laid the foundation for the bureaucracy to become incorporated, as a means of survival, into the state structure, where it became an appendage of the government (particularly the State Department). The payoff for the bureaucracy was considerable. On the one hand, through their complicity in the witch hunt and deals with employers, they were rendered safe from attack by the rank and file; on the other hand, the government-sponsored, cannibalistic raids against "red" unions provided the additional members needed by a bureaucracy incapable of expanding into unorganized spheres.

Increases in productivity have long since become means of erosion of the working class, for the unions have inadequate contractual defenses against the elimination of jobs by new machinery, and they possess no program whatsoever for protecting the rights of laid-off workers. The introduction of automatic equipment and computers has already played havoc with railroad workers, miners and others, and is capable of wiping out several trades during the next few years. Still, the union leadership stubbornly clings to its base among high-seniority workers. Transformed into job-trusts, the unions seek only pensions, productivity bonuses, retirement pay, etc.—all those fringe benefits that primarily benefit the higher-seniority workers.

The introduction of modern machinery and industrial rationalization by corporate management since WWII has largely eliminated skill differentials between workers as the basis for wage differentiation. The new labor aristocracy in the industrial plants, therefore, derive their benefits and privileges mainly from seniority. Originally a means of protection, seniority is now the basis for new divisions within the working class. Seniority carries with it higher wages, better (easier) jobs, protection of jobs and conditions, and incentive pay. Younger workers are often left with little or no representation. In the International Longshoremen's and Warehousemen's Union, a casual labor pool keeps them out of the union; in steel plants, a pool for lower-paid workers keeps them out of seniority units.

These labor pools, and other divisive forms of organization of the industrial work force, such as the long probationary periods in the auto industry, have created virtual caste divisions in which younger workers form a *cushion of super-exploitation for the employers, partially compensating them for the privileges granted to older workers.* This superexploitation extends into the lower strata of the workers formally represented by the unions, as mechanization and automation, rather than ameliorating the tedious routine of mass production, create greater opportunities for increasing the intensity of labor.

The lower-waged newer workers, therefore, are paying for the wage increases (usually graduated into percentage increases), the fringe benefits, and the pensions for the high-seniority employees.

The most exploited sections of the class are now differentiated by age, sex and race. Young workers, Black workers and women workers constitute the bulk of workers outside the unions or reduced to second-class status within them. The once-radical older unionists today constitute the most privileged and hence the most conservatized section of the working class.

Is there any hope for American labor?

The white male, skilled, high-seniority worker, with his economic and cultural privileges, is indeed a "beneficiary" of the system, yet he is nervous and apprehensive about automation and he mistrusts the labor bureaucracy. He recognizes, by and large, the contrast between his immediate interests and those of the unorganized, underprivileged and unemployed mass, and he is acutely aware of the role the union plays in preserving and deepening this contrast. The basic traditions of unionism—solidarity, equality and struggle—linger on, and, despite everything, there is usually a militant, old or young, in every shop and every office.

A whole set of actual and potential factors portend the revival of old militancy: the necessity of capitalists to confront the working class with far greater demands upon their self-sacrifice than were imposed even during World War II; the whip of fascist reaction; pressure from the revolutionary Black movement; the example of the coming labor party and revolutionary union developments in the South; and the pressure of a growing revolutionary cadre that could be created today from forces which are ready now, but are largely outside the unions.

Still, the tide of docility, cynicism and helplessness will

not be easily turned. The technological revolution demands a revolutionary labor movement to wrest gains instead of reverses from cybernation, and the extant organized labor movement cannot rise to this level under its present leadership. The AFL-CIO apparatus is both bankrupt in policy and unrepresentative of the broad working class. The radicalization of the organized labor movement requires, therefore, a titanic explosion within the unions, and the current tendency of unionists to challenge the bureaucracy is only a precursor of this coming eruption.

In the final analysis, the source of a labor revival will be the youth, along with Black and female workers, who constitute the most exploited section of the working class. Their deteriorating conditions of labor will engender in them an affinity with the growing political movements in the country outside the union movement, and they will find ways and means of penetrating the consciousness of the militants within the unions and stimulating them into motion.

A realistic approach to the class struggle in the United States today provides little ground for syndicalist illusions. Organized labor will, in all likelihood, be the last social formation to go into motion, and a labor party emanating from the unions—the great hope of the early days of the CIO—cannot be expected to be the next major step in the arena of independent class political action. A mass base for independent politics is already developing from other directions. The tempo and scope of the radicalization of such forces as the Mississippi Freedom Democratic Party, the Freedom Now Party, radicals regrouped around China and Cuba, defiant students, etc., will modify the need for and the nature of the labor party.

The very survival of labor organizations requires that a new revolutionary wing in the unions emerge. The initial impulse for this formation will come from people and issues within the class but outside the unions, rather than from economic issues within the union. The success of a new revolutionary wing in the unions will ultimately depend upon the impact by the revolutionary socialist party which calls for the left wing, and upon its ability to propel toward the unions those workers already radicalized in areas outside the jurisdiction of the labor bureaucracy.

The ultimate fate of the remaining unions is intimately connected with their racial structure. The ability of a union to survive and reverse its degenerate trend depends in large

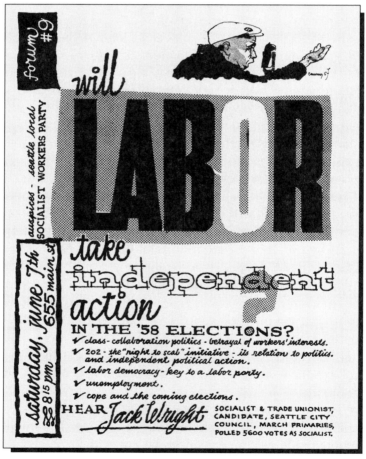

Leaflet for 1958 Seattle SWP forum. (Drawing by Pacific Northwest artist William Cumming)

measure on its racial composition. There are one million Black workers in the AFL-CIO today, a unique sector of the working class—a transmission belt between organized labor and the class struggle outside the unions. Unions with a sufficient Black membership will be sensitive to the pressure of the fascist movement which basically aims to extend the southern political system throughout the country. And as the southern worker-Black leadership clarifies its aims, it will have a decisive influence upon at least those unions retaining sparks of viability.

In the '30s, radicals believed the labor movement would "save" Blacks. Today, the role of savior-leader is reversed: the climate of militancy surrounding the struggle of the dark-skinned people is contagious; it cannot help but affect the unions and to a certain extent it already has. But Black workers can no more save the present union structure than they can the Democrats or the system; political democracy, a decent living standard and strong unions can only be won and sustained in the context of a struggle for a Workers and Farmers government. As the bloody battle for integration passes over into the fight for socialism, attracting to its ranks the most oppressed and most conscious elements of society—Black militants, youth, women, the unemployed and marginally employed, the impoverished aged, rebellious students and intellectuals—the trade unionists will move.

The *race* question has always been a dominating issue of American politics, and it is the key to the great problem confronting us today: how will the gap be bridged between employed and unemployed, Black and white, young and old? It is the civil rights struggle that encompasses, embodies and represents every other oppressed grouping, whose best representatives identify with the Black liberation struggle. Freedom Now becomes the voice of the exploited everywhere, and the force that knocks at the door of the privileged elements of the class, demanding their support on the basis of principle, solidarity and their own frustrated needs.

Black and white rebels from the outcast ranks of the affluent society, organized by and around the Black movement because there is no other institution in their lives that can organize them, are the forces who will shape the direction of general workingclass motion, eventually pressing the most exploited and aware sections of organized labor into action on behalf of their own grievances and the common misery of the class. In the process, a combined and fused leadership will emerge.

The coming pre-revolutionary situation

The existence of a mass revolutionary force of Black people within the economic context of an approaching general crisis indicates that the coming period in the U.S. will be pre-revolutionary.

In 1938, Trotsky placed the U.S. in a pre-revolutionary situation by virtue of the rise of the CIO. Black proletarians are a more objectively revolutionary social formation than even the CIO sit-downers of the '30s, because the status quo is intolerable to them, and yet their most elementary problems cannot be solved within the system. The major demands of the labor movement in the '30s were won and consolidated, but only social revolution can establish racial equality. Furthermore, Blacks, as an objectively revolutionary people, must operate in the most conservative majority milieu in the world. The volcanic nature of this contradiction stamps the Black struggle as the most profoundly revolutionary movement in the world.

The impact of Black radicalism has thus far primarily jarred youth, radicals, women and the church (due to the "new breed" of clergymen fresh from campus or pressured by the Black ministry). As the leadership of the civil rights movement matures, a chain reaction in the working class can take place, and we will witness the northern workers, in turn, mobilizing against speedup, unemployment, injustice, fascism and war.[45]

Part 2
Leadership

This analysis was originally published as "Radical Labor-ism versus Bolshevik Leadership," a pre-convention discussion bulletin coauthored by Clara Fraser (Kaye) and Richard Fraser (Kirk) for the 1965 SWP Convention.

The opening paragraphs refer to main developments in the SWP leadership since the 1950s. In the early years of that decade, a decisive political battle was fought against the Cochranites, who advocated dissolving the party and entering Stalinist organizations.[46] With luminary SWP leader James P. Cannon in semi-retirement, defense of the party fell to the new regime led by Farrell Dobbs and Tom Kerry.[47] Dobbs and Kerry took on the Cochranites halfheartedly, for reasons discussed in this chapter. In the years that followed, they drove out the principled, pro-Cannon tendency led by Murry Weiss and Myra Tanner Weiss,[48] and destroyed the party's internal democracy and revolutionary integrity. The political trajectory of Dobbs and Kerry, described in detail in the following pages, was maintained by their successor, Jack Barnes, leading to the SWP's explicit rejection of Trotskyism in the 1980s.

Character of the present leadership

Thirteen years have elapsed since the fight with the Cochranites.

Until 1961, the stewardship of the SWP was nominally held jointly by the current regime and the Weiss group leaders. With the elimination of the Weiss group, the Dobbs-Kerry group entrenched itself and established a political monopoly of the leadership.

What are the principal achievements of the existing leadership since consolidating themselves?

1. The withdrawal from Cuba defense work and from trips to Cuba designed to break the travel ban.[49]

2. The reduction of the once-independent youth to a chattel of the SWP National Office, and the prolonged insulation of these youth from the ferment around them in the general student movement.

3. The removal of all political-minority representation on the Political Committee; the avowed intention of destroying all minority formations, pockets and opinions in the party at large; and the tidal wave of expulsions on ephemeral grounds and in an unprecedentedly compulsive manner.

4. Recurrent disasters in our relations with the northern Black struggle and an absolute self-segregation from the southern struggle that is indefensible, especially on the incredible organizational grounds of "no forces available."

5. Rejection of obvious and principled opportunities to enlarge the party through serious fusion, regroupment or united front tactics.

6. Chronic organizational and political intimidation of all party advocates of the emancipation of women.

7. Ignominious default in regaining ideological hegemony over the radical movement, rationalized away by the canard of an absence of qualified personnel to accomplish this.

8. Refusal to assume organizational initiative of any kind in any mass movement, and the corollary of elevating basic organizational tasks of the party (fund-raising, subscription drives, paper sales) to the plane of political crusades, thereby reducing party life to internal maintenance plus election campaigns.

It is time to inquire into the nature of a leadership which has basically undermined the interventionist and democratic traditions of the party, and yet appears before the party with complacency and with an Organizational Resolution that validates everything it has done and then proceeds to shake the big stick at the remaining party dissidents.

What is wrong with the regime?

An analysis of its history and modus operandi leads inescapably to the conclusion that the present leadership is *Radical Laborite* in character and not Bolshevik.

It is Laborite because it believes that socialist politics on an extended scale will develop exclusively through the medium of a labor party based on the unions. It is Radical because of the powerful residue of the traditions of revolutionary socialism in the party.

In its social origin, the regime derives from the militant AFL unionism of the '30s, and its vision does not basically project beyond the trade union upsurge of the distant future that will lead to the labor party. This myopia lends an anti-political cast to its view of reality.

Not typical syndicalists, nor anti-party in the Cochranite sense, the regime nevertheless does not intervene decisively in the *real political life of the time* so long as the arenas of struggle and motion remain outside the labor movement and sometimes opposed to it. The regime permits participation in other movements (in a grudging response to pressure from party branches in the field) but the "participation" proposed by the center is a follow-the-leader adaptation to the prevailing winds of whichever movement strikes its fancy at a given time. When controversy develops, as it must, within these movements, the word is usually, "Get out!"

The rigidly unionistic framework of the regime's long-range strategy results not only in non-intervention but in a deep-rooted, anti-theoretical habit.

As a consequence of the single-minded unionistic-laboristic blueprint for revolution, the party has become increasingly constricted, rigid, conservative and turned-inward. This produces, in turn, deepening errors of theory, program, strategy and tactics in those areas demanding the greatest familiarity and precision of evaluation: the colonial revolution, youth, the peace movement, the Black struggle, the labor movement, women's emancipation and revolutionary regroupment.

The chief characteristics of the Radical Laborites, then, are fourfold: they are non-interventionist, contemptuous of theory, union-bound in strategical orientation, and politically unstable in their reactions to any given juncture.

Non-interventionist

Exclusively focusing on the strategic variant of the labor party, the leadership is generally impervious and insensitive toward non-unionistic facets of the class struggle, and where it must evaluate the radical developments of any stage, it is inconsistent and ambivalent, apparently disinterested in fundamental (rather than reportorial) conjunctural analyses and the tactical shifts (other than inspection tours) indicated by conjunctural changes.

The regime recognizes struggles other than large union upheavals for general propaganda purposes only. Somewhat like the Socialist Labor Party clinging to its fetish of Socialist Industrial Unionism and riding out a half-century with election campaigns and journalistic commentary, the SWP seems resigned to a pattern of reporting and general socialist education.

The vital problems and needs of the newly developing vanguard groups in the country are treated superficially; except for correctly urging them to independent political action, the *Militant* has no more advice for them than the *National Guardian*, which approves them all, or the *Weekly People*, which is contemptuous of them all.[50]

What should Malcolm X have done? What should the Student Non-Violent Coordinating Committee and the Mississippi Freedom Democratic Party do? Students for a Democratic Society? Progressive Labor Party? What next for the campus teach-ins? What program for women? Doesn't anybody have to do anything before the unions move? Evidently not. Evidently no current development involves urgent *political* problems, demanding direct intervention, initiative and agitation by the SWP.

Today's real and potential mass movements are considered interesting but secondary and subordinate phenomena, and their groping leaders are viewed by the SWP with an uncritical blindness which sometimes borders on adulation, or with excessive political suspicion and competitive organizational mistrust.

Compounding the error, the regime also neglects probes into the unions, preferring to wait until the time is more patently promising. Comrades working in unionized shops are instructed *not* to appear as "union politicians" but to concentrate on recruiting to the party. Not only is this a false polarization of interdependent activities, but the logic involved would force the party not to conduct election campaigns on pain of being labeled "Establishment Politicians"—an accusation frequently made against us which we constantly have to explain.

And today we must explain it again to the party leadership: wherever we are, we are revolutionary politicians working within extant structures in order to either change their policies or overthrow the structures themselves. If it is tactical to work within the framework of the *bourgeois state* via election campaigns, how downright sectarian it is to fear the guilt-by-association charge engendered by working within the framework of the degenerated class organs of the proletariat—the union movement!

We are not spectators of the internal union processes from within the unions; wherever our organizational participation in the union provides us a rostrum for principled propaganda and agitation, we would be foolish to abjure it.

It is significant that the Political Resolution stresses our "propagandistic" nature and tasks, while the Organizational Resolution mentions the multitudinous areas of participation and intervention supposedly characteristic of our party and evidently supposed to be maintained.[51] But this is a liturgical chant only. Business will proceed as usual, and intervention will be cooled off and discouraged wherever possible. The present projected "intervention" in the youth antiwar movement, for instance, will produce as few lasting results and political continuity as did our participation in Fair Play for Cuba Committee, Committee to Aid the Monroe Defendants,[52] Freedom Now Party, etc., because the orientation to mass work is either politically wrong or tactically superficial.

Anti-theoretical

Coming forward in the struggle against the petty-bourgeois intellectual opposition in 1941,[53] and helping to defeat it, the present Dobbs-Kerry leadership gradually converted our suspicion of middleclass intellectuals into a rejection of all theoreticians in politics.

The Dobbs-Kerry regime tolerates "theory" on foreign affairs which do not deeply concern it—China, Cuba, the International—and on questions of abstract philosophy, which are not troublesome as long as they remain abstract. But any encroachment upon its domestic territory by a minority viewpoint is promptly labeled—intellectual! The word has become synonymous with "oppositional" and with "petty-bourgeois" and is used as an insult.

The dialectical interconnections of the Leninist concept of worker-Bolshevik, Marxist-intellectual, organizer-theoretician, etc., have been summarily split in two by the regime with the separate parts reassembled into new units. Theory/ideology is now the exclusive function of the regime, while the ranks and the organizers are expected to work at sub drives, fund drives, forums and campus activities, period. Naturally, this "leave the thinking to us" law results in very little thought by anyone at all.

Minorities are answered not with logical political disputation, but with muddying distortion and fabrication of the issues, invective and personal-organizational attacks. Political arguments used to be serious and educational experiences for the entire party membership; today, any consistent or persistent theoretical, strategic or tactical difference provokes a reflex characteristic of the labor officialdom, echoing its intolerance, prejudices and sewer terminology.

Contempt for theory breeds an inability to tolerate criticism, and both traits are expressed in the anti-intellectualism of the radical laborites.

Neo-economist[54]

The Dobbs-Kerry leadership is the second major negative tendency closely associated with labor unionism to appear in the SWP in the postwar period.

Between the present leadership and the Cochranites an obvious affinity existed, marked by the reluctance and tardiness of the Dobbs-Kerry break with Cochran. However, an important difference exists between these two factions.

The Minneapolis Teamsters Union and the Sailors Union of the Pacific (and Marine Firemen) were the first two mass labor bases won by the SWP and they produced the present leadership of the party.

These unions, not as socially and politically advanced in terms of overall program and ideology as the newer CIO unions, were nevertheless extremely militant in their pursuit of job benefits and resistance against government intervention into the unions.

They were therefore among the first objectives of the employer-government drive to housebreak the labor movement. The Teamsters came under fire immediately before World War II and the Sailors Union of the Pacific shortly after the war. The hierarchies of these unions joined forces with the bosses and the state to drive out the radicals, and the struggles which ensued forced a sharp and decisive break between the SWP and these unions, cutting off the present SWP leadership from its base of mass support.

The Cochranites, on the other hand, were still more or less firmly entrenched, mainly in the United Auto Workers, in 1951. They were propelled away from the party because they had a mass milieu and mass base to lean on and escape into as the witch hunt became general.

Centrist?

Of recent years, several opponents of the Dobbs-Kerry leadership both within and outside the party have characterized the majority as Centrist. The prevalence of this term requires an evaluation of the regime with respect to a definition of the word.

The Dobbs-Kerry regime does reveal definite political deviations from revolutionary criteria.

1. The regime certainly flirts with reformism in three areas.

Their approach to the Black question is reformist, as most glaringly revealed in the curious proposition that All-Black political action is the solution to the race question in the North while "Troops to the South" will raise the political level of Blacks there.

Secondly, the party regime has substituted the "30 hours work for 40 hours pay" slogan for Trotsky's sliding scale of wages and hours, instead of connecting them.[55] While 30-40 is an important demand to press, and may obviously have positive consequences, it still does not, by itself, necessarily constitute a bridge from reformist to revolutionary consciousness. On the contrary, it may become a means of strengthening reformism at a given stage. And in sectors of the economy undergoing automation, the 30-40 slogan doesn't scratch the surface of the vast unemployment problem.

Thirdly, the very barrenness of the Political Committee's current Political Resolution, void of either conjunctural analysis or revolutionary perspective, holds the door open to further flirtations with reformism.

2. The political reflex of the leadership to critical events and shifts is demonstrably non-revolutionary.

Forceful intervention by comrades Cannon and Graham was needed to rectify the hands-off, Third Camp policy adopted at the outbreak of the Korean War.[56]

The political line during the Cuban missile crisis was at best ambivalent and at worst bordered on joining the anti-Soviet hysteria, only from the "left."[57]

The regime betrays an obsession with "security" (as in the Cuba trips) which more often than not attempts to mask an unsure policy. Their unseemly concern with respectability occasionally veers toward panic, as evinced after the Kennedy assassination, revealing marked instability, impressionism and legalistic defensiveness.[58] The *reductio ad absurdum* of this approach was performed by the Young Socialist Alliance leadership when it issued national mimeographed instructions to its convention delegates, including married couples, forbidding them to "shack up" with each other because of "security."

3. The disinterest in and hostility towards any movement for women's emancipation reveals another facet of the basically non-Bolshevik outlook of the present leadership.

All right. Do all these enumerated weaknesses add up to centrism?

Trotsky defined centrism as an *unstable political formation in motion between reformism and Bolshevism.*

The source of motion in centrism is to be found largely in external social forces which exert both reformist and revolutionary pressures. But the one thing which clearly characterizes the SWP leadership is its ability to insulate itself from all external pressures by means of a rigid sectarianism.

Isolated from *both* the reformist and revolutionary pressures exerted by the mass movements, it is subject to the direct pressure of the capitalist class, with no counter-pressure from the mass movements.

The effects of this pressure have been thus far insufficient to cause *motion* in the SWP; rather, a certain stagnation grips the party and its leadership.

If and when the SWP majority relates itself to the existing mass movements, and permits itself to feel and react to the contradictory and alternating pressures generated there, its true and definitive political character will emerge. Life will show whether the present indefinite state of the core of the majority signifies centrism. Everyone, in fact, will be tested under these conditions.

Meanwhile, we do not yet see that the political designation of centrism has an important bearing on the problem of party leadership in the SWP today. More important at this moment and decisive for the future are its sectarianism, self-insulation, irrational suspicion of new vanguard formations—particularly anything emanating from the CP milieu or the South—and insensitivity to the problems and struggles of the most oppressed.

These traits derive not so much from centrist faults as from a Laborite-Economist reflex operating in the period of a *degenerating* labor movement.

Actually the regime has not changed very much in the past two decades. Vast changes in the objective situation have simply exposed another side of its character.

Strategy of the holding operation

This is a state of suspended animation which freezes program and cements the cadre in a decades-long cliffhanging position until the resurgence of organized labor—the main question—is at hand. Then, the party is supposed to drop down to *terra firma* and move in. The present "tightened-up" propagandistic activism is only a new form of the basic holding operation, designed to make it palatable to energetic youth.

This self-paralysis and self-segregation, this marking time and treading water, is constantly being disturbed by the

STRATEGY OF THE HOLDING OPERATION

pressure of changes, turns and crises provided by everyday events. The economy gyrates in abrupt swings and cycles, social relations shift, and political repercussions accumulate; the rhythm of revolutionary politics, like that of life, is the rhythm of the seesaw. But the regime will not be provoked into altering its freeze-in; it equates programmatic firmness with the posture of the spectator and tries to modulate and modify the significance of every development to fit its own long-range timetable.

Its perspective and schedule, however, based on a concept of relatively uneventful evolution, leave no room for relating to the leaps and twists of the real political world. The regime hopes to see a growth in the party from small to big to bigger, and then, someday, on to Power. Unfortunately, such a smooth and predictable progression is not in the nature of things, as the German Social Democracy came to learn. Behind the welfare state facade of U.S. capitalism lie a voracious imperialism, the Mississippi police state, the Vietnam War, etc., all producing cataclysmic reactions. It is possible to keep one's head and balance only if the chronic imbalance and inbred surprises of the system are appreciated and anticipated as the norm. But the party is rocked and disoriented at virtually every new and unexpected juncture because it is not geared to dialectics, materialism or political flexibility.

The very nature of monopoly capital dictates the swift sequence of widely varying conjunctures. A fixed program that does not grow, and a petrified long-range strategy that persists no matter what, are results of contempt for the changing winds of reality. The SWP today has asserted its superiority over the basic laws of political motion: it promises that hanging on, hanging tough, waiting it out and letting the struggle *come to us,* is sufficient for eventual victory.

In a revolutionary period, we expect the masses to intervene in their own destiny. We expect a revolutionary party, however, to be doing this *all the time.*

Non-democratic centralism

A non-interventionist, anti-theoretical, laboristic and legalistic regime conducting an unnecessary holding operation can maintain itself only by tightening centralism and diminishing democracy. So Dobbs and Kerry proceed to maintain themselves precisely through bureaucratic means, flagrantly violating Leninist organizational principles and practices.

A long history of internal conflicts paved the way for the present distortion of SWP organizational traditions.

The expulsion of Field, who thought the party would permit him to adapt opportunistically to the pressure of the mass movement, established the authority of the party over its mass workers.[59] The expulsion of Zack reinforced this principle and affirmed the right of the Political Committee to intervene directly in the branches.[60]

The debate with Oehler over the "French Turn" (entry of Trotskyists into the leftward-moving Socialist Party in France and elsewhere in the mid-30s) established the polar unity of organizational flexibility and programmatic firmness as the required foundation for relations with centrist groupings.[61]

The struggle against Abern isolated and exposed the disease of clique politics and organizational combinationism.[62]

The consuming and paralyzing daily battles with the Shactmanite petty-bourgeois opposition necessitated formalizing internal discussion by placing constitutional limitations on it.

The fight with Morrow in 1945-46 established the Control Commission.[63]

The main thrust of our advances toward democratic centralism was to acquire a much needed degree of centralism. However, this centralism is now in the hands of an anti-political tendency which uses it to reinforce its monopoly of leadership. Our heritage and tradition of democracy, that *other* part of democratic centralism, are being steadily eroded.

The Nominating Commission

One example of the ongoing erosion of democracy is to be seen in the recent practices of the Nominating Commission.

Conceived by Comrade Cannon as a bulwark of the rank and file to protect itself against a self-perpetuating leadership, it has turned into its opposite. It has become a means through which the central leadership entrenches itself and its friends without having to take responsibility for proposing this. The Commission perpetrates vendettas against opponents, who may suddenly be dropped from the National Committee without any discussion or explanation; a previous understanding with large voting blocs accounts for this phenomenon, which contemptuously ignores the form, procedure and spirit of the proposal which created the Commission.

The Control Commission

This Commission has similarly changed character.

Shortly after the last convention, a lengthy Control Commission report was submitted of an investigation of considerable duration, undertaken quite awhile before the convention. This "investigation" of the Milwaukee Branch, was conducted largely by Political Committee appointees. The actual members of the Control Commission, however, dutifully signed the report—an unprecedented, slanderous report that rebuked the organizer and the branch unfairly and illogically. The Control Commission members did not personally investigate, interrogate witnesses or determine the direction of interrogation. No report was made to the convention of this investigation.[64]

The Control Commission behaves as a non-responsible body, i.e., not responsible to the party. It is incumbent upon an outgoing Control Commission *above all other bodies in the party* to make a full report of its activities to the convention. But had this been done, even majority supporters might have objected to the unusual procedure of the Political Committee relegating to itself the function of the Commission.

War against political minorities

In his speech to the New York Branch on the expulsion of Robertson, Comrade Dobbs claimed that the expulsion (which had provoked widespread criticism from all sectors of the party) illustrated Comrade Cannon's dictum that principle has primacy over organizational questions.[65] These are empty words. What Cannon meant was one thing, but all these words mean in the new context is that the leadership pretends to be justified by tradition in expelling anyone it can first outvote on political questions

An even more disturbing proposition was placed before the party in this speech. Comrade Dobbs justified the expulsion on the grounds that it was a mistake in the first place for Robertson to be allowed into the SWP. We do not invite enemies into the party, he said. This sinister statement was Dobbs' way of making two other points:

1. He established the "principle" that any kangaroo court proceedings constitute a fair trial because the real purpose of the "trial" is to rectify the mistake that allowed an enemy to exist within the organization. And how is enemy status determined? By whomever the majority can outvote. And since any minority can be outvoted, any minority is the "enemy"—solely by virtue of being a minority.

The logical outcome of this new principle is obvious: no more minorities in the SWP.

2. The Robertson expulsion was calculated to be an epitaph on the political gravestones of those "politically irresponsible" elements who "invited" the enemy into the party in the first place. So, Robertson was only a relatively innocent bystander, representing a handy vehicle for the repudiation of regroupment, the old Cannonism, and Murry Weiss, who recruited Robertson from the Socialist Party

with the full approval of the rest of the SWP leadership.

An unprecedented number of threats and disciplinary actions against members of various minorities, on clearly secondary grounds, and often for unclear and even spurious reasons, have occurred from coast to coast:

1. Comrade Arne Swabeck, a leading party theoretician, was prevented from giving a public talk.[66]

2. High pressure "suggestions" have emanated from various branch leaderships that worker comrades resign.

3. Threats of expulsion or being dropped for "lack of activity" are prevalent in many branches.

4. An entire branch (Milwaukee) was censured for expelling a common thief.

5. Expulsion has resulted for comrades privately expressing disloyal thoughts. (Robertson group.)

6. Expulsion has resulted because comrades made an unavoidable press statement, or were guilty of "unauthorized" participation in a mass demonstration. (Robertson group.)

7. The Detroit branch placed Comrade Art Phillips on charges for failure to participate in a sub drive at a time when he was conducting a long and bitterly fought union struggle in his UAW local—and at the very outset of the pre-convention internal discussion in the party. His fate reveals what is projected for the future:

a) No minority opinion will be tolerated.

b) The class struggle has been decreed outside the area of acceptable party "activity." *Proletarians will become increasingly unpopular in the SWP.*

The new school of socialist discipline

As discrimination and prejudice against political minorities and unionists harden and a strange new organizational climate prevails in the party, young activists are being trained to become branch organizers of a different and special type. Organizational "hard-liners" and super-activists, they are encouraged to transform their branches into tightly controlled "combat" units, ruthlessly stripped of all "fat," "deadwood" and dissidence.

The present campaign for "tightening up" the party is being undertaken at the branch level by this new stratum which never had a chance to learn the real meaning of democratic centralism. The new leaders have been taught to equate centralism with monolithism, and democracy with unprincipled, social-democratic all-inclusiveness.

The new young activist-leadership energetically procures revenue, organizes literature distributions and keeps branch wheels turning. All of this is highly commendable, necessary and basic. However, they have been endowed by the majority leadership with virtually unlimited authority over all areas of party activity in quite a few branches, and their high-handed methods are being unfortunately endorsed by some "old-timers"—another new term of contempt—who are intimidated by the image of omnipotence projected by the new leader-technicians.

These new super-disciplinarians operate in the ideological image of the central leadership and attempt to emulate it in every way. They are largely, nevertheless, petty-bourgeois, stemming from an essentially middleclass student origin. Consequently, the scare tactics they deploy against "nonactivists" (usually political dissidents) tend to introduce a *class* friction into party relations similar to that fomented by Gould, Glotzer, et al.—the hard core of the petty-bourgeois intellectual opposition in 1940.[67] But one key difference prevails: the present student youth leadership, mimicking the majority leadership, tends to be an *anti-intellectual* petty-bourgeoisie.

This is not to say that the mis-educated young socialists in the SWP are responsible for the regime. No—they are its captives. The central leadership, and its close supporters, have ordained the course of the party, and it is they who control the party. An ingenuous youth may counter the charge that the SWP is making a satellite out of a youth movement with the rejoinder, "But the youth runs the SWP!" Nevertheless, the youth in its present form has been molded by the SWP regime and the excesses of the youth—sterility, rigidity, conservatism and harshness—are clear harbingers of things to come in an SWP finally rid of the last vestige of "disloyalty."

Except for the lies, deceit and manipulation of organizational minutiae involving political minorities, the organizational practices of the leadership do not often appear to be illegal. But a higher criterion than formal legality exists: the dialectics of democracy and centralism in the service of a revolutionary policy, i.e., principled politics. There are no constitutional provisions which defend the party against unprincipled politics, yet this is the fundamental organizational basis upon which a regime must be judged.

Unprincipled politics

The present organizational document before the party, purportedly drawing the lessons of the last period, studiously ignores the most tortuous organizational convulsion of the decade: the destruction of the Weiss group, and how and why it was driven from the party.

The fundamental political-organizational axis of internal party life since the Cochranite split in 1953 (aside from the Marcyites, who were a party unto themselves)[68] was the reciprocal relation between the central leadership and the Weiss group, and their counter-relations with the Wohlforth-Robertson group.

Any resolution on organization which avoids discussion of this conflict is an abstraction. The present resolution does not scratch the surface of the organizational question in life, except to re-exhibit the leadership's flair for evading concrete reality.

The "Weiss group" comprised virtually an entire generation, at that time a younger generation, in the secondary leadership. They were loyal activists with a deep theoretical interest, particularly in the relation between theory and practice. They stood for principled politics and for interventionist tactics.

The relentless annihilation of this group and its reduction to the status of nonpersons in party history are the crowning achievement of the present regime and the basis of its consolidation and impetus. The effective purge of the Weiss group is supposed to be a demonstration of superior politics—how to achieve the destruction of an opponent in a "soft" split. Yet not one word about how this marvel was accomplished appears in the resolution.

What are the words? They exist and they aptly describe the process: unprincipled organizational combinationism. An old malady of American Trotskyism, this practice has hardened into a habit of the central leadership and has become typical of its relations with party minorities ranging from Cochran to Wohlforth.

Basically unconcerned with theory and program, the regime cynically consummates organizational deals with its political opponents at the expense of its political allies.

The regime helps organize the Cochran faction

The Weiss group was in the forefront of the struggle against Cochran after he declared war on the fundamentals of Trotskyism in 1952. Comrades Dobbs and Kerry at this time were in close organizational alliance with Cochran. Even though they were in basic political agreement with Weiss and rejected Cochran's revisionism, they refused to defend the Weiss group "intellectuals" and "professional revolutionaries" whom Cochran was fiercely attacking.

Instead, Comrades Dobbs & Kerry helped organize the Cochran faction in at least the Seattle Branch, where

Dobbs, in person and on the scene, conferred official approval upon the factional organization of an absolutely unprincipled combination of Cochranites, Bartellites, and Marcyites. Dobbs then proceeded to encourage the new faction to undertake a power struggle against the branch leadership on purely organizational issues. He even reported back promptly to the appalled majority faction this bestowal of his blessing on an anti-party group, justifying it on the grounds that his national post demanded that he be "fair, impartial and democratic."

Only after nationwide resistance to Cochran-Clarke was generated by the secondary leadership and membership did the central leadership reluctantly break its unprincipled bloc and help repel Cochran's struggle for power.

The regime protects Wohlforth against himself

Eight years later, when Wohlforth and his anti-Cuba faction were leading the youth, *Comrades Dobbs & Kerry consummated an organizational agreement with him which prohibited any opposition to him from youth comrades loyal to the Cuban Revolution and in firm support of SWP policy on Cuba.* In spite of this unwarranted deal between the leadership and Wohlforth, many youth comrades felt they had to defend the Cuban Revolution among the youth and they entered into a struggle against Wohlforth.

Comrades Dobbs & Kerry threatened disciplinary action against the loyal youth for breaking the calm of their unprincipled bloc with Wohlforth. Challenged by Comrades Murry Weiss and Dan Roberts, and prevented from pursuing their unprecedented course by the plenum of the National Committee (1961), they withdrew their charges against the majority youth. But in a shocking revenge maneuver, several of the loyal SWP youth were eliminated from the National Committee by means of the silent blackballing technique used by Dobbs-Kerry adherents on the Nominations Commission.

When open discussion of the Cuba question finally isolated Wohlforth among the youth, the majority leaders who had initiated the fight against him and who were therefore the logical candidates for youth leadership were bypassed. A new leadership was manufactured, the chief criterion being loyalty to the SWP regime.

This signified the end of the organizational independence of the youth, the end of the attempt to develop a self-reliant youth leadership, and the end of the Weiss group—as a result of its demoralization over the outrageous tactics wielded against it.

The regime punishes the wrong man

After this disgraceful "victory," possibilities for the continued exercise of unprincipled politics were by no means exhausted. *The final relations of the regime with Wohlforth-Robertson* add a fitting postscript to the history of the Weiss group.

The main grievance of the Political Committee against the Wohlforth-Robertson minority was that they were agents of Healy.[69] But Robertson and Wohlforth then split because Robertson refused to take orders from Healy. Did this not create a new and more favorable relation between Robertson and the Political Committee (the New York leadership)? By all the criteria of principled politics, it should have. But Wohlforth was willing to maneuver with the Political Committee. He had previously informed on Robertson about petty matters to camouflage his own continuing ties with Healy, and he expected a payoff. He got it—*Robertson* was expelled and Healy's agent remained, until in his own good time he chose to be expelled.

The fundamental modus operandi of the regime—unprincipled politics—has prevailed for 13 years and is now deeply ingrained. The unparalleled conduct of Comrades Dobbs-Kerry is connected to, and a product of, their grim antagonism to the Weiss group.

The Weiss grouping

What was the source of the antagonism to the Weiss group and why have the differences been suppressed so long by both sides?

Not until after the liquidation of the Weiss group were any hints of political differences between the two groupings manifested in major resolutions. At the 1963 convention, Comrade Myra Tanner Weiss proposed some amendments to the Political Resolution. But long before this, there existed differences and shades of difference which the Weiss group minimized or repressed after the Cochran split in the interests of building a unified collective leadership on fundamental questions.

The differences

The sources of friction were threefold.

The Weiss group held to *theory* as the fundamental guide of the party.

Objectively, their *interventionist* bent and tactics constituted resistance to the holding operation.

Finally, they were outspoken proponents of *women's emancipation* in society and in the party.

On all three counts, the anti-politicals considered them a menace.

Theory

The Weisses were teachers of basic Marxism. They conveyed a deep respect for theory and for the worker-Bolshevik concept of the party member. They wanted a party of revolutionary intellectuals, of thinker-doers. This led to a concern with maintaining a constant relation between theory and practice, and between strategy and tactics. This in turn led to a habit of leadership accountability and responsibility, in the sense of Trotsky's constant demand upon leadership to be *self-critical*.

This tradition has vanished from the National Office. As

impressionism and eclecticism replace theory in the SWP, the doctrine of leadership infallibility and immunity from criticism prevails. The need for leadership to regularly present a candid and complete *balance sheet* on past policy and performance is honored only in the breach. Political errors of the Dobbs-Kerry machine are either ignored or incorporated into party doctrine as vindicated appraisals and actions.

Interventionism

The Weiss group, in contrast to the Dobbs-Kerry holding operation, characteristically sought SWP influence within any leftward-moving currents.

This required strategical talent, but such talent was typical of party leadership in the formative years of our movement. Flexibility, alertness to opportunity and initiative were the political skills bred by early Trotskyism.

The 1956 regroupment campaign symbolized this spirit of the old "Cannonism," but the real and lasting gains achieved by that campaign were written off by the present regime precisely because of its hostility to any such turns. It wants no more maneuvers and negotiations with *groupings*—large or small, centrist or revolutionary. It orients only to untainted individuals without dangerously lurid pasts.

Women's emancipation

The defense of women's rights is a particularly irritating matter to the regime. Their testy reflex to this issue exposes their non-communist character, for they wish to build a party in which the average backward worker will immediately feel comfortable.

In regard to race prejudice in the party, Comrade Vernon wrote that white radicals are justified in creating that type of party climate in which white workers would feel at home, even though Blacks are repelled:

Radicals are fully aware of the politically reactionary aspects of American policies and condemn those aspects of American life which they can pinpoint as direct products of capitalism per se, but are basically in harmony with what passes for American culture, and identify with the American (i.e., white) people. They had better. Their job and goal is to get closer to and fuse with the American workers and people, and this requires being American.[70]

We answered him in 1963 as follows:

> Vernon is both stunningly right and fortunately wrong. He is right in his enumeration of the qualities estranging Negroes from us; he is wrong in thinking our bad habits are good socialist tactics.

> We *are* isolated from the white working class. We are isolated because of our revolutionary program and principles. No amount of conformity to cultural mores or anything else will compensate for this, and our isolation will prevail until objective conditions force a change in workingclass opinion. However, our concessions to the general illiberal folkways of white America do estrange us from its key victims—Negroes, women, youth—leaving us very isolated indeed.[71]

Lenin warned that the revolutionary party must not encompass any of the backward prejudices of the proletariat. He called upon men and women Bolsheviks to heed the plight of oppressed women and aid them in the party and in society.

Almost alone among SWPers, Comrade Myra Tanner Weiss heard Lenin's call and responded to it, educating and re-educating members of all generations in regard to the vital theoretical, political and organizational significance of the woman question.

Her reward, of course, except for the gratitude of the few, was the hostility of the many, accompanied by demagogic downgrading in typical male chauvinist style. She is

Farrell Dobbs and Myra Tanner Weiss were SWP running mates in 1952, '56, and '60. (Cover of campaign pamphlet)

subjected to blatant insult and condescension, an approach that is most effectively undertaken by women defenders of the regime—best exemplified in the article "An Answer to M.T. Weiss' 'Comments'," by Hedda Garza, in the Internal Bulletin.[72]

This is how the SWP deals with the comrade who was its

foremost female spokesman for 20 years. The SWP does not educate against male chauvinism, it agitates against real women leaders.

The "soft" split

The gap between Weiss and Dobbs-Kerry grew out of the unspoken question, *"What kind of a party shall we aspire to be?"*

The old communists, Lenin and Trotsky, aspired to build parties of people who hate capitalism, want to destroy it and will fight for freedom and fraternity in and out of the party.

Bolshevik circles were always marked by a distinct atmosphere of *equality*. Workers, intellectuals, men, women, different nationalities, the aged, the youth, and adherents of many diversified viewpoints on many issues all lived together in mutual respect and collaboration. The leadership was clearly multi-tendency and operated *collectively*. Democratic centralism was the glue that held them together, and democracy was *never* sacrificed to centralism until the necessities of War Communism clearly demanded it. Indeed, the argumentativeness of the Bolsheviks was an international joke, but these disputatious Russians were the people who led the first successful proletarian revolution in history.

The atmosphere of equality repelled those who could not or would not accept this criterion for party membership. In the SWP, however, Bolshevik practice is reversed and everything is stood on its head. A clearly revolutionary aggregate of leaders, the Weiss group, was driven from the SWP precisely because the Dobbs-Kerry faction would not tolerate even *vague* tendencies within the leadership.

The Weiss group was demoralized by discriminatory treatment and unabashed vindictiveness. It was possible for them to virtually fall apart under the lash of persecution because of two factors:

1. They never published an analysis of the political char-

acter and social background of the very leadership that was factionally organized against them. They thereby helped prepare their own victimization.

2. For all their devotion to theory, they could never bring themselves to look critically upon party *doctrine,* which included Negro Nationalism and the label of "secondary" applied to both the Black and Woman questions as a matter of *principle.*

About a year after the Cochranites left the party in 1953, the branches suddenly received a National Office communication signed by Murry Weiss, then functioning in the central New York leadership. He was calling upon his supporters, who "perhaps" constituted a clique, to disband. He "repudiated" any past unconscious leadership of a clique.

What specific pressures and rationalizations evoked this *Darkness At Noon* "confession" and self-slander can only be surmised.[73] In general, however, this capitulation was predicated on the conviction that unity on the Political Committee must be maintained *at all costs*, and that to raise any issue other than the most obvious and elementary which-side-are-you-on question was diversionary and disruptive. At bottom, he had no confidence in the necessity and ability of the National Committee or the party ranks to call the regime to order.

Comrade Weiss' reluctance to speak out until it was too late stemmed from his lack of a clear-cut programmatic differentiation, his commitment not to rock the boat, and an attitude of futility about the possibility of change within the party. Certainly, the methods and programs of the regime are supported by the majority of the party, due to the fact that 1) the clique politics of the regime are obscured by the peculiarity that the *clique is the regime,* and 2) the erratic conjunctural and episodic reflexes of the leadership appear to have the blessings of the founders of the party.

But the discussion of controversial ideas within the party cannot be repressed forever, and open discussion cannot always await the pleasure of the leadership. *The lid will blow as yesterday's disputed or suppressed "secondary questions" become the burning issues of the day (as they usually do).* When the obsession over preserving the unity of the leadership congeals into the paramount organizational concern of all the various tendencies within that leadership, Leninism is no longer a living reality in the movement and internal education comes to a dead halt. It is not open controversy that breeds divisive centrifugal tendencies, but precisely the repression of political controversy for *organizational reasons*.

The SWP is paying the price today for the myopia of that sector of the leadership which recognized the incipient dangers to the party but instead of giving serious analytical thought to them, willingly created window-dressing for the suspect regime.

When Dobbs-Kerry saw the opportunity to establish a machine that would insure them total control of the party, the Weiss group became superfluous and had to go.

The "soft" split—the secret, puzzling, non-event split—will haunt and taunt this party indefinitely until it is understood.

The concealed years: transitional stage to the new course

The issue of the "soft" split has been easily and readily relegated by many people to past history, as if party history played no conditioning role in the character of the organism today. Newer and younger comrades are taught to view SWP history as interesting but irrelevant, and comrades with more seniority have long allowed the masquerade of a consensus to play on and on, even when they recognized stunning departures from principled traditions and practices.

The analysis of the real differences between Comrades Weiss and Dobbs-Kerry serves to inform and remind us that the past epoch has indeed been relevant. It was one phase in the *process* of the SWP, an interim marked by growing counter-currents to the predominant trends of the pre-Cochran epoch. These counter-currents have now crystallized.

The nature of the Weiss group was a negative indication of the nature of the Dobbs-Kerry group. The latter inoculates the membership against those very traditions of American Trotskyism which demonstrated in life how a small, but correct, Bolshevik party could grow and prosper. Devotion to theory, programmatic clarity, scientific conjunctural analyses, interventions, fusions, splits, principled politics and organizational flexibility—all are consigned these days to the realm of old junk, necessary in the dim past when all we supposedly did was sit in cellars, read the books, and clarify theory, but outmoded today when what is needed is *"Action!"*

Action? Even words have been changed to connote their polar opposite meanings.

Of what bold thrusts does this new "Action" consist? Let us see. Literature promotion, fund drives, and a tightened organizational structure devised to isolate and confine those who oppose the new course. Evidently nothing more is needed because our future leadership of the American proletariat is ordained.

But this leadership, alas, is not ordained. It depends precisely upon what we do. And what the SWP is doing, apart from basic tasks of drives, elections and education, is wrong —wrong in strategy, tactics and evaluation of life both within and beyond 116 University Place (the National Office).

The regime may keep its eyes glued to the AFL-CIO ball, but radical life moves outside and around the unions, bypassing and outstripping them for the present as viable organs of mass action. New areas of vital action emerge in the country and new serious contenders for radical leadership appear. The party is faced with new problems and new opportunities, but these are largely ignored. The party is likewise faced with the need to confront and settle long unresolved and even unnamed disputes.

But when the living history of the party becomes substance not for illumination and education, but for awkward silence and crass distortion, it grows increasingly apparent that the concealed years and the unreported struggles contain the clue to the real political nature of the regime, the barrenness of its program and the blatant deviationism of its organizational policies.

The Organizational Question

The Political Committee's Organizational Resolution, the subject and product of a special plenum of the National Committee, provides the legal cover for administrative practices already in effect. The document is a mopping-up operation, formalizing the high-handed methods typical of the regime.

One of the myths promulgated by the leadership is that it is "unprincipled" to criticize them on organizational procedures 1) so long as political differences do *not* exist, and 2) so long as political differences *do* exist!

There is no precedent for this fantastic formula anywhere in the revolutionary movement. The tested law of principled politics that organizational grievances not be raised ahead of and in place of extant political differences has become thoroughly distorted.

Relationship of programmatic and organizational issues

In the fight with the petty-bourgeois opposition in 1940, Trotsky and Cannon promised to deal minutely with the organizational question *after* the political issues were resolved, and this they proceeded to do. Still, an aura of suspiciousness surrounds organizational proposals and objections that arise from outside the central leadership itself. Members of the party objecting to violations of past practices are told, in effect, to develop a faction on the question of Outer Mongolia or keep quiet, because organizational criticisms are *always* supposed to represent deeper or unconscious political differences.

So the ranks are prevented from criticism so long as they do not have political differences, and conversely, if an avowed political faction or minority raises organizational questions or protests organizational practices which they believe are in violation of their rights, they are promptly damned for "obscuring" the political questions and "introducing" trivia.

It is time to take issue with the falsity, hypocrisy and downright unfairness of this nonsense. Insistence on programmatic issues taking precedence over administrative issues arose from pre-factional situations where anti-party tendencies refused to reveal their full program and had to be smoked out. *No such minority has congealed in the SWP since 1953.* Every faction in the past decade has explicitly and directly announced its points of ideological difference.

Existing factions have every right to voice their opinions about the regime, complain, or criticize administrative conduct without being demagogically condemned for doing so. And comrades who believe themselves to be in political agreement with the majority or who do not know what, if any, programmatic differences they may have, possess not only the right but the responsibility to express themselves critically on organization matters at any time.

Some minority factions, like the Marcyites and Johnsonites,[74] further away from the majority than any of the contemporary minorities, never voiced objections to the methods and practices of the regime. Indeed, *they had no cause to.* The leadership always bent over backwards to accommodate them, integrate them into the party and the leadership, and extend to them every democratic avenue of expression.

These fortunate minorities did not abuse their privileges,

either, and generally behaved with restraint and respect for the rules.

Similarly, many comrades in the past decade have seriously questioned one or a number of practices of the regime and have never developed political differences.

The Organization Question is not *just* and not *always* a reflection of and a link to programmatic questions. It also has an identity and a character of its own. The party has a right to judge the leadership *on this question alone.* It is neither honest nor principled for any leadership, whether on a national or branch level, to demand of a critic that he anchor his objections in *Capital* before he can be heard.

If his objections are indeed anchored there, the regime has no right to denounce him as unwarranted, petty or extraneous if he raises any protest over administrative issues affecting him.

In the final analysis, the Organization Question, in addition to having an identity of its own, is itself a *political question,* and politicalized comrades should stop denigrating it. They tend to consider organizational matters as unworthy of their attention and intervention because of the second-class status of the issue. Exclusively concerned with wondering if *their* organizational objections have deeper political roots, they completely forget that *the organizational practices of the leadership may have deeper political causes than the leadership cares to reveal.*

It may well be that the new pogrom of expulsions, suspensions, censures, threats, etc., is powered by *a different concept of the party and SWP program* on the part of the leadership, a concept that the regime obscures by its convention resolutions which, in most cases, appear to reiterate traditional positions of the party.

Surely, a regime that openly threatens to get rid of certain branches and individuals—even "active" ones!—and warns that it will "clean up" certain areas and "eliminate factionalism" for all time, is a regime to whom the following question may validly be addressed:

"Comrades, just what is your *political* program and strategy for the SWP? And how can party *organizational* practices change so radically unless they are actually rooted in your undivulged new politics and perspectives?!"

Leadership accountability

The spectacle of a regime that brands as "disruptive" an organizational protest by a political minority that has a real or suspected grievance is a sorry spectacle, rife with hypocrisy. The regime has the responsibility of answering criticism by admitting or denying it and has no right to "reject" it. It may postpone discussion of the issue, but to turn majority-minority relations into bourgeois diplomacy-style gamesmanship is to reduce leadership responsibility for its organizational practices into nothingness.

Most branch organizers know this, and know as well that they are capable of plenty of mistakes, excesses, myopias, and general underachievement! Still, they are accountable for their stewardship. That the central regime should somehow stand exempt from the necessary criteria and norms of judging leadership and assume the mantle of absolute organizational and procedural inviolability from criticism—taking exception to the *form* rather than the *content* of criticism—is a mockery of the very democratic centralism they claim as their guide.

Factional showdown in the party corral

It is apparent from the new Organization Resolution that the regime isn't quite sure how far to go in proscribing factions. Nor is it at all sure what kind of an organization it presides over.

The Political Resolution tells us that the SWP isn't even a party but is still a *propaganda group*—but the Organization Resolution promptly transforms us into a *combat party* mobilized to seize state power!

The Political Resolution tells us that our tasks are *propagandistic*—but the Organization Resolution decrees more centralism so that we can more effectively *penetrate* the mass movement!

It is difficult to know whether absent-mindedness, inefficiency, cynicism or schizophrenia is at work here. One can only admire a leadership which not only defends its position but defends two mutually exclusive positions with equal zeal.

In regard to factions, page 15 of the Organization Resolution assures us that "The right to organize tendencies and factions is safeguarded." Very nice, exemplary, properly traditional. But hold on—pages 16 and 17 describe in Grand Guignol terms exactly what you can expect *after* you exercise this dubious "right." A faction cannot be politically justified we are told, *unless* it conducts a power fight! Furthermore, if differences are so fundamental as to justify the organization of a faction, then the faction "must" conduct a "showdown fight for control of the party."

Fantastic. Not only does the regime now have the right to commandeer private factional correspondence, it has the audacity to order factions to conduct "war against the party" on the pain of being labeled "politically unjustifiable" if the factions do not declare war!

This is to serve notice on the party majority that the Seattle Branch of the SWP refuses to foment a power fight, and if this be disloyalty to the new "Organizational Character of the SWP" as well as proof of our "disruptive" and "degenerate" nature, let the Political Committee act forthwith.

So factions are evidently still legal but politically immoral, unwise, unnecessary and provocative *by their very nature*. Faction members are not necessarily criminals (unless they refuse to incite splits) but they are definitely irresponsible fools and knaves, ordained to become anti-party cliques.

Dissidence outlawed

The Progressive Labor Party (PL) convention, scorned by the *Militant*, was much more consistent. *Because* factions are evil, they said, they are prohibited; in their place, "criticism and self-criticism" shall prevail. The *Militant* dismissed this as "Stalinist garbage." But what alternative avenue of criticism does the Political Committee propose for PL or for itself? If factions are anti-party and if individual criticism is garbage, what are the approved outlets for dissent?

We are repeatedly told in the Organization Resolution that "ample room is provided for the expression of dissident views." Where? When? How?

Every two years, the convention decides policy for all questions that will arise during the next two years, even surprise events that haven't happened yet, like the Kennedy assassination, Cuban missile crisis, etc. Since criticism can only be advanced and (supposedly) discussed during a three-month pre-convention discussion period every two years, then anyone planning ahead as to how best to intervene in this discussion with a minority viewpoint is vilified as a factionalist because he is organized and/or hasn't changed his mind since the last convention when he was only a tendency.

Furthermore, while anyone may certainly *express* critical views at the convention, hardly anyone can get them *discussed* objectively and on their merits. Distortion and insult have displaced political debate in the SWP.

In life, then, *no real room is provided for objective and serious discussion and debate* of dissident views. All critics are promptly slandered, pilloried and obscenitied. For many long years, the SWP had the enviable and unique reputation of being a democratic centralist party that permitted factions and factional life, but today, opposition on any question whatsoever has been rendered so suspect, so disgraceful and so dangerous to its formulator that scenes like the following are commonplace:

A party leader speaks in diametric opposition to a Political Committee resolution at a national convention. Then, to the bewilderment of some unsophisticated delegates, he votes *for* the PC resolution—because, he says, you just don't vote against the leadership!

So much for the regime's habit of pointing with pride to the "overwhelming" majority vote and the "minute" votes garnered by minorities. In life, to vote against the regime in order to register your opinion is intolerable disloyalty that disqualifies comrades from first-class party citizenship.

The "ample room" for critical expression is equivalent to the choice of the last meal by the condemned man.

The current regime forces dissenters into becoming tendencies and tendencies into becoming factions. The only alternatives are abject capitulation, despite one's convictions, individual withering away, or, ironically, that very phenomenon about which the regime waxes so righteously indignant—degeneration into cliques. The history of the Communist Party should serve warning on the SWP: where factions and political disputes are overtly or in effect prohibited, cliques will proliferate, serving as private formations for the discussion of burning party issues.

The absurd contention that factions mean power fights is a political frame-up and the formulation should be summarily removed from the resolution. It is designed to prejudice any discussion of political questions raised by an organized minority. It illustrates one of the fundamental characteristics of the regime: when faced with political opposition, it promptly creates hysteria in the party over secondary organizational questions. This allows the regime to evade defending its policy in the "objective," "responsible" and "educational" manner piously advocated by the resolution, and still attain its objective—an "overwhelming" majority vote.

Both Lenin and Trotsky bequeathed to us the unchangeable right to organize factions for the express purpose of trying to influence and persuade the membership *and* the leadership to alter or adjust party policy. There is not one word in the doctrine of Bolshevism to the effect that the majority is by nature correct and the minority automatically wrong. Yet according to the present Organization Resolution, "basic differences with the party line" are caused by "alien class pressures...ideas, moods and motivations at odds with our program and traditions...nervousness translated into exaggerated criticism of the party...those who develop basic political differences also develop an urge to throw off restrictions imposed upon them by the party's organizational concepts. They become antagonistic to democratic centralism."

The self-critical spirit of revolutionists

This "analysis" of minorities is not only a shameful generalization but an ignorant political error. It assumes that nobody knows that Marx, Engels, Lenin, Trotsky and Cannon were frequently in minorities themselves. The regime really believes that party line is equivalent to absolute truth and minority opinion equal to absolute "capitulation to alien class pressures"—but that the entire party believes this is unbelievable! Surely, even among those who have not become so "disoriented" as to organize factions, somebody has absorbed the rigorously self-critical spirit of Marxism as described by Marx's biographer, Franz Mehring:

> If Marx and Engels were alive today they would certainly have nothing but biting contempt for the suggestion that the merciless criticism which was their sharpest weapon should never be turned against themselves.
>
> Their real greatness does not consist in the fact that they never made a mistake, but in the fact that they never attempted to persist in a mistake for one moment after they had recognized it as such.[75]

The Organization Resolution buries this spirit once and for all, for not only has the Dobbs-Kerry regime never made a mistake, it is self-described as generically incapable of making any. The majority, therefore, by automatically supporting the regime, will always be historically right.

There aren't enough Organizational Resolutions in the world to continually suppress the factions forced into being by such a hallowed leadership In *The History of American Trotskyism,* Comrade Cannon writes:

> Once a movement has evolved through experience and through struggle and internal conflict to the point where it consolidates a body of leaders who enjoy wide authority, who are capable of working together and who are more or less homogeneous in their political conceptions, then faction struggles tend to diminish. They become rarer and are less destructive. They take different forms, have more clearly evident ideological content and are more instructive to the membership. The consolidation of such a leadership becomes a powerful factor in mitigating and sometimes preventing further faction fights.[76]

The consolidation of such a leadership is devoutly to be wished. Obviously, it has not yet materialized in the Socialist Workers Party.

Appendix 1
A Transitional Program for the Southern Revolution

For a second Reconstruction of the South

Constitutional law—the Bill of Rights—for the South; the present states have no legal right to recognition as part of the U.S.

For an independent freedom party— the Freedom Labor Party

As the labor party concept recedes in the North, it comes forward in the South as the only exact designation of the *content* of the real movement there. Linking up the civil rights struggle with the socio-economic needs of the southern working class as a whole will energize the revolutionary drive of all sectors.

The attempt to organize sharecroppers and farm laborers into unions is an inevitable product of the political organization of the southern masses, as has been demonstrated in Mississippi. It is also inevitable that the Mississippi Freedom Democratic Party will become a genuine interracial movement in the process.

The vast difficulty of organizing unions under the police-state regime will demonstrate to the poor white his need to solidarize with the civil rights movement, which represents a struggle for his civil rights as well.

Unions created by oppressed southern workers will be unions of a new model, unhampered by the conservatism of the northern labor movement and capable of intensive political and revolutionary actions.

The living labor solidarity of the new unions would constitute the basis of the Freedom Labor Party.

Towards dual power

Expand the Freedom Ballot. Elect Freedom Labor regimes in every state, demanding recognition by the federal government and Congress as the only lawful bodies of the South.

The skeleton of dual power already exists. The MFDP refuses to recognize the legality and validity of the power structure in Mississippi; it is organized to challenge and supplant this power, and it knows that the showdown will take place in the street, and probably against federal troops.

Defense guards for the Freedom Ballot

As the organized protective apparatus of the dual power, Freedom Ballot defense guards can become the workers' militia of the next stage of the revolution. It is essential that these bodies be controlled by the Freedom Labor Party. Careful study should be given to the development and successful operation of the Deacons self-defense movement in Louisiana. These are the embryonic forms of the workers' militia.

Destroy the police state

A basic political change is required to bring constitutional government to the South, but the police state cannot be reformed. The ballot in the South is a sham today, and continued participation in the plebiscites of the state is fruitless. A break with reform is necessary. The police state must be overthrown. The present power structure must be labeled for what it is, eliminated, and replaced by the new power of the victorious masses.

Appendix 2
Statements in Support of the Southern Freedom Struggle

A memorial to Congress

Petition circulated during the 1964 elections by the Freedom Socialist Party, a Left electoral coalition which included the then-Seattle Branch of the SWP[77]

WHEREAS, the fundamental defect of American democracy has been its inability to bring the rule of law to large areas of the South, causing the citizens of these areas to live in constant jeopardy of life and liberty at the hands of lawless elements, and

WHEREAS, this lawless condition is supported, maintained and perpetuated by the whole Power Structure of the South, whereby there is no rule of law but of arbitrary violence secretly organized by Klans and Councils and supported by the State and local governments and police, constabulary, courts, judges, sheriffs, jailers, executioners and other public officials, and

WHEREAS, after the Civil War, the working people of the South, Black and white, under the protection of the Union Army, did establish and maintain governments of a democratic character which, for the first and only time in the history of this area, gave protection of citizens under the Bill of Rights and the 13th, 14th and 15th Amendments, and

WHEREAS, these governments were deprived of Federal protection by illegal, secret and subversive agreements between the Democratic and Republican parties (the one most publicly exposed being the Compromise of 1877), and by this means the democratic regime was subjected to violence and terrorism which finally achieved the overthrow of these governments by lawless elements under the banner of White Supremacy, and

WHEREAS, the present State governments of the South are the direct products of this violence and terrorism and unlawful overthrow of constituted democratic authority, and as a result of their origin and of the police-state and fascist methods by which they have been perpetrated, there exists neither Freedom of Speech, Freedom of Worship, Freedom of Assemblage, Freedom of the Press, the Right to Vote, the Right to Trial by a Jury of Peers, Protection against Illegal Search and Seizure, the Right of Due Process of Law, the Right to Petition for Redress of Grievances, nor any of the substantial rights of the individual to which, according to the Constitution, all American citizens are entitled; nor do working people have the right of collective bargaining, a right which cannot exist without a foundation of all the above Constitutionally guaranteed rights, and

WHEREAS, this lawless Southern System has had profound influence on culture and practices in every part of the country, and furthermore, through various individuals and organizations and under the sponsorship of powerful capitalistic interests, tends to extend itself throughout the U.S. and thereby constitutes a grave danger and threat to the civil rights and liberties of all, and to all democratic institutions including labor organizations, places of worship, political organizations, etc., and

WHEREAS, there is no legal framework in the Southern system of lawless government whereby change toward a constitutional form of government might be initiated, and

WHEREAS, Article 4, Section 4 of the Constitution requires the Federal Government to guarantee to every State a Republican form of government, and

WHEREAS, there can be no Republican form of government without the freedom of citizens to exercise the above mentioned rights, which are denied to whites only to a lesser degree than to Blacks,

BE IT THEREFORE RESOLVED, that we, the undersigned citizens, do hereby memorialize the Congress of the United States to place the people of the Southern States under its protection as did the great 39th Congress, and proceed to bring these areas under the rule of law by the following measures:

1. That in the states of North Carolina, South Carolina, Georgia, Florida, Alabama, Mississippi, Louisiana, Arkansas, Texas, Virginia, Tennessee and Kentucky, the Congress of the United States shall declare that there exist no legal governments.

2. That no Congressmen chosen under these State governments be seated in either the House of Representatives or the U.S. Senate.

3. That all State and local governments be required to disband, and all police, constabulary and other military bodies created under these State governments be disbanded and disarmed.

4. That law and order be maintained by a voluntary Peoples' Militia which shall be constituted by those citizens who have proven their respect for Constitutional law by their struggle against the Southern police state. This Militia shall be operative until such time as a republican form of government may be restored to such areas and guaranteed for the future.

5. That full rights of citizenship shall be proclaimed for all citizens of the age of 18 or over, except those proven to have participated in the suppression of human and Constitutional rights.

6. That the States of New Mexico, Arizona, Maryland, Delaware, Oklahoma and West Virginia, and the southern parts of Ohio, Indiana, Illinois and Missouri, be placed

under probationary status for six months, during which time they must establish the full authority of Constitutional law under pain of similar measures as are applied to the first aforementioned States.

7. That all areas where Constitutional rights are in any way violated, including specifically large Northern cities, Indian reservations, and areas of large-scale agriculture, shall be immediately investigated, and drastic measures, consistent with the above principles, be taken to assure the immediate and unconditional rights of persons throughout the land.

Protest against the Washington State candidates' loyalty oath

1964

This oath, which I hereby sign under protest, is a violation of the republican form of government which is guaranteed to the citizens of the State of Washington whereby the citizens are legally entitled to make their democratic choice of all candidates who may wish to come before them.

I sign, however, only with the understanding that nothing in this oath shall prevent me from pointing out to the electorate, while running for Federal office, that the people of many Southern states are totally deprived of a republican form of government by the existence of police states controlled only by Klans and Councils and other lawless elements and not by the people, and that if the people of these states should be forced to resort to revolutionary means to establish a republican form of government, that I, as a representative in Congress, or as a candidate for such an office and a refugee from said police states, would consider it a betrayal of the United States Constitution to fail to support them.

WAYMON WARE,
Freedom Socialist Party Candidate for Representative,
Seventh Congressional District of the State of Washington

Statement to the 1964 Democratic National Convention

by the Seattle branches of the Socialist Workers Party and the Young Socialist Alliance

Support the challenge instituted by the Mississippi Freedom Democratic Party against the seating of the illegally elected Congressmen from Mississippi!

Demand the seating of the MFDP candidates—the only candidates from Mississippi elected by a general franchise and able to take the oath of office to uphold the Constitution!

Extend the challenge to all Congressmen illegally elected from the Southern States!

MFDP: a great achievement

The creation of the Mississippi Freedom Democratic Party as the independent political arm of the Southern fight for freedom is the most important political achievement of the current movement for civil rights in the South.

For the first time in this century masses of Southern Negroes and their white allies braved the terror of the police and the Klan in order to vote for a party dedicated to the overthrow of the Democratic Party in Mississippi and the system of terror, segregation, poverty and enforced ignorance maintained by it.

Ninety-five thousand Mississippians, mostly Black, supported MFDP in a "mock" election in 1963. In 1964, when they slackened their independent character and included Johnson-Humphrey on their ticket, MFDP received about 65,000 votes.

Mississippi Democratic Party is part of the national party

The elections not only demonstrated the tremendous support available to MFDP as an independent party, but the valid skepticism of Southern freedom fighters about the good intentions of the national Democratic Party.

At the 1964 Democratic Convention, MFDP exposed the national party as supporter and prop for Southern tyranny. The Johnson-directed Democrats preserved federal patronage and support for the Mississippi racists by refusing to seat the delegates elected by the MFDP in an open unsegregated convention.

It is, of course, common knowledge that the alliance of Southern congressmen controls both houses and has a representative in the White House. But MFDP forced Johnson and the Democratic National Committee to reveal that its Mississippi party is part and parcel of the national party and is courted and maintained by it.

Attempt to bury MFDP

Moreover, the national Democratic Party is intent on completely destroying the independence of the MFDP. Through liberals and rightwing supporters and participants in the civil rights movement, it has pressured MFDP into dropping its valid claims to the seats of the Mississippi congressmen it is challenging. Spokesmen for MFDP have even made claim to being the true representatives of the Democratic Party in the South and the upholder of its program.

Such a claim is foolish and self-defeating. The Negroes in Mississippi did not brave police terror in order to win the discrimination and prejudice maintained by the Democratic administration and its Northern parties.

The Democratic Party stands opposed to any principle of humanism to which the MFDP is committed. The racist, antilabor, redbaiting, militaristic and imperialist-minded Southern congressmen are the true image of the national Democratic Party. They are the principal supporters of Johnson's imperialist assault on Vietnam and the Dominican Republic; they fully endorse the racist attack on the Congo; and they are not greatly disturbed by Johnson's hypocritical, demagogic, and mostly rhetorical support to the fight against segregation.

The claim that the MFDP is the legitimate Democratic Party in Mississippi plays into the hands of the administration and its agents who are intent upon maintaining peace and the status quo in the South by sidetracking the struggle for power in Mississippi into a fruitless and debilitating fight within the Democratic Party.

The program to enter the Democratic Party plays into the hands of the KKK. The racists are the founders of the Democratic Party in the U.S. They control it in partnership with big business interests, and the idea that they will be purged out in the interests of democracy in the South is the greatest hoax ever perpetrated by American liberalism.

The MFDP has nothing to gain from capitulating to the administration liberals. The Democratic Party never has and never will declare racism illegal.

Road to victory

But the Mississippi Freedom Democratic Party need not be dependent upon the national Democratic Party. It can make great strides for freedom in the United States by:

1. Deepening its program of political and economic revolution in the South and thereby winning the support of the oppressed whites as well as the Negroes.

2. Extending its campaign throughout the Southern states, where millions of disenfranchised and exploited Negro and white workers will support a challenge of the fascist-like regimes directed by the Democratic Party.

3. Clearly establishing its independence from the Democratic Party and its national and international policies, and linking its demands with the needs of the people.

4. Clearly demonstrating that they are not merely out to expose or change the Democratic Party, but to take power from the racists and establish representative government in the South for the first time since the Reconstruction.

Appendix 3
Founding Documents of the Freedom Socialist Party

Statement of resignation from the SWP
April 9, 1966, Seattle, Washington

It is a tribute to the genius of Leon Trotsky that the movement he founded could survive in the U.S. so long after his death, during two long decades of prosperity, world domination and relative quiescence in the working class.

Nevertheless, the once proud SWP, the hallmark of international solidarity and revolutionary intransigence, has become a movement eroded in program and perspective. The events of the past few months, culminating in the February plenum of the National Committee, constitute a nodal point in a long process of political decline.

The degeneration of the SWP majority is acutely revealed in the utter lack of theory and conjunctural analysis which marks its approach. The method of the majority is eclectic impressionism, and the policies flowing from this are sterile and contradictory, resulting in false positions on the Negro struggle, the key domestic problem of the era, and on China, the key international problem of the revolutionary movement.

Incapable of any economic evaluation of the current status of U.S. imperialism, the majority's domestic politics consist of a flirtation with reform on the issue of the Vietnamese war, and a view of the coming upsurge of labor as a "single-issue" type of process, connected to no other social struggle extant or developing—such as the Negro struggle, women's rights, youth and the poverty-stricken.

The majority's strategic preoccupation with the trade unions as the exclusive medium of social transformation expresses itself in a conservative sectarianism towards the protracted ideological ferment in both old and new radical circles, as well as in a hardened contempt for the efforts of women and youth to emancipate themselves from oppression.

Just as the Socialist Labor Party petrified around the conjunctural evaluation of the 19th century Marxists, so the SWP has ossified around its conjunctural evaluations of 25 years ago. It is today either oblivious or wrong about the main political problems and needs of our epoch.

We have sought to offset this degeneration by a series of struggles on central political questions.

I. The Negro struggle

For 15 years, our tendency has pressed for theoretical clarity on this *central question of the American revolution*. We have urged that a deep analysis of a unique phenomenon replace the present policy of superimposing the doctrine of European nationalism upon the Negro question here.

In a series of documents presented for internal party discussion (particularly three convention resolutions on the Negro struggle in 1957 and 1963 by Kirk, and the Kirk-Kaye Political Resolution in 1965), we have emphasized the objectively revolutionary nature of the Negro struggle *as it is* and we have labeled its course as "Revolutionary Integration."[78]

A powerful Negro cadre might have been built around this program, for it provided the basis for meaningful intervention into the southern struggle, the civil rights movement in the North, the ghetto battle, and the growing ideological controversy raging in the Negro movement today.

But the party majority insured that none of these documents were discussed objectively in the party. When the central leadership condescended to reply at all, it was principally with falsification and caricature of our position, spiced with organizational vilifications.

When, in 1957, we criticized the majority's uncritical adaptation to Rev. King and to pacifism, we were accused of *over*-estimating the independence of the Negro struggle. When, in 1963, we opposed the over-adaptation to Mr. Muhammad and the glorification of separatism, we were accused of being white so-called radicals or liberal reformists who *under*-estimated the independence of the struggle. For our part, we considered the party line opportunist and tail-endist in both instances.

The majority is responsible for a series of unprecedented disasters in its relations with the Negro movement, defeats that have completely isolated the party from the key upsurge of our time and yet have never been explained. Today, with the southern movement in deep programmatic crisis, and the northern ghetto on the verge of explosions which will rock American society to its foundations, the party has less contact with, understanding of, or orientation to this struggle than at any time in the past 25 years.

The self-confidence of the party in its ability to alter its racial composition has accordingly been shattered. *The SWP has become crystallized as an essentially white party,* and it lacks the impetus to alter this condition.

It bequeaths the Negro struggle to the petty-bourgeois nationalists and the middleclass tokenists, thereby cutting the party off from the resuscitating effects of the class struggle and deepening its withdrawal from reality.

The SWP now presents the ludicrous spectacle of a lily-white party with a program of ultra-black nationalism. The adulation of the Muslims has opened a Pandora's box of violations of elementary workingclass principles: SWP spokesmen now justify the nationalists' discrimination against women, their anti-Semitism, and their collaboration with fascists.

Finally, it is the majority which adapts theoretically to

the liberals on the Negro question. Perhaps the last act in the tragedy of the SWP and the Negro struggle was Comrade Camejo's pseudo-historical, pseudo-economic YSA Bulletin article where he categorically stated that the bourgeoisie will implant Northern-style democracy in the South.

This proposition has only been implied in party resolutions since 1957; now it is doctrine, and nothing could be better calculated to promote the absolute alienation of the party from the Negro struggle than the categorical denial of the permanent revolutionary character of the Negro struggle for integration.

The overestimation of the vitality of the bourgeoisie, endowing it with a revolutionary vigor it was unable to summon even during Reconstruction, is the result of the method of economic determinism, and it will lead to further ideological retreats on fundamental questions of American politics.

II. *The colonial revolution*

We have called for political solidarity with the Chinese Revolution. Despite bureaucratic deformations and Stalinist baggage, it is the key to the colonial revolution and a central axis of revolutionary politics throughout the world. But the SWP has cut itself off from relating to the dynamics of this great revolution.

Just as the majority mechanically transfers European nationalism to the Negro question in the USA, so it exports Stalinist degeneration in the Soviet Union over to revolutionary China, and concludes with the strategy of political revolution in China.

Instead of concrete socio-analysis, inappropriate labels like "Stalinist" are pasted over the Chinese regime and the SWP conducts a frantic search for every apparent Stalinist-type deviation in Maoist policy and practice. The dialectic of a living revolution that has evolved into ever-intensifying opposition to the Kremlin is totally ignored, and in place of enthusiasm we are offered scorn.

In Cuba, on the other hand, the superficial evaluation of Castro's attack on Trotskyism, Gilly, China, etc., reveals the tendency of the majority leadership to cling to Castro as to a life-preserver, ignoring the obvious basic shift to the right and toward the Soviet bureaucracy.[79] The job of class analysis and solidarity with the Latin American proletariat against Castro's shift is left to the Chinese leadership and to—Healy.

III. Vietnam

The current attack upon the Kirk-Kaye tendency results directly from our advocacy of a proletarian antiwar policy that would solidarize the party with the revolution in Vietnam, with the workingclass Negro youth who are key victims of the draft in the U.S., and with the left wing of the antiwar movement.

As we stated in our letter rejecting the National Committee's censure of Kirk for having the audacity to attempt a discussion of party antiwar policy:

> We ought to bring about a critical consideration of the strategy and tactics employed at the Thanksgiving CC [National Coordinating Committee to End the War in Vietnam] conference in Washington, D.C.,[80] where YSA and SWP, by insisting on a "single-issue"-oriented movement, served to arrest the radicalization of the New Left and effectively isolated themselves from the revolutionary wing of the southern Negro struggle.

> We also opposed their sectarian insistence on forcing all conference activity to circulate around a purely organizational struggle to isolate the independents in a new organization, when the burning responsibility for YSA and SWP was to conduct a clear political struggle against a SANE-liberal-CP conspiracy to disorient the antiwar movement.[81]

SWP policy is divorced from any economic and social analysis of the current crisis of U.S. capitalism. We have maintained that the capitalist class has a fundamental stake in this particular war, and will not quit short of military/political defeat in Vietnam, or virtual civil war at home.

The majority calls for "withdrawal" as against "negotiations" are obviously correct. But under cover of this lurks the essentially pacifist proposition that the antiwar movement can, with its own forces, pressure the U.S. out of Vietnam. And it is a fundamental of Trotskyism that pacifism, translated into political terms, is reformism.

The flight from Marxism takes place when the vanguard element in the antiwar movement and in the New Left are groping for fundamental solutions to social problems, seeking to unite Negro freedom fighters, the poverty-stricken, the opposition to the draft, and the antiwar movement in one broad political movement against the war. The SWP turns the radicalization of the New Left over to the CP and to the pacifists, and thus to the Democrats, and then lauds its own "realistic" aloofness from the burning problem of the antiwar movement.

It is typical majority slander that we advise the party to turn its back on the student movement in favor of the Negro movement. We urge the revolutionary youth to struggle for political leadership on the campuses. However, the militant students whom we lead must be encouraged in their groping for alliance with the proletariat, and in their growing feeling that only the workers have the capacity to stop this particular war. Antiwar youth must turn toward the working class—and specifically toward the Negroes, who are that section of the class already in motion.

The SWP's "single-issue" gimmick is a false answer to a false posing of the movement's problems, and it acts in life as a conservative barrier to the political maturation of young militants.

IV. *The regeneration of socialist thought*

Our tendency quickly grasped the significance of Khrushchev's exposure of Stalin, and Seattle Branch had singular success with its campaign to recruit dissident CPers to Trotskyism.

But the SWP majority was unprepared to discuss two of the burning questions confronting the advanced CP cadres: CP policy of Negro self-determination, and the Chinese challenge to the Soviet bureaucracy. The SWP could not, therefore, intervene with full effectiveness in internecine struggle in the Communist milieu and could not stimulate a national leftwing in the CP.

As a result, the fruit of regroupment work belongs to other organizations.

Progressive Labor Party has grabbed off a left wing of the Communist Party. Spartacist has a left wing of the Socialist Party. And a whole galaxy of centrist-type youth and adult tendencies has appeared.

We have tried to orient the party toward this general leftward stream emerging under the impulse of world events, but the party pretends that no such large and fluid milieu exists. The SWP is still mired in the holding operation, which is a prolonged state of suspension based upon the assumption that nothing significant can really happen until the regeneration of the trade unions and the emergence of the labor party.

Chained to the fixed idea that the SWP is automatically ordained as the leadership of the future, the majority is in the grip of a conservative sectarianism which views all new socialist formations and developments with hostility from the very outset. The organizational flexibility of the old Cannonism is junked and a rigid enmity to all new "competition" ensues.

And yet, without the intervention of Trotskyism, the new currents will stop short of revolutionary Marxism and will petrify in centrism.

V. The Woman Question

Ours is the only tendency in the history of American Trotskyism to place the struggle for women's emancipation on the level of a first-rate theoretical and programmatic question. We have vainly resisted the creeping paralysis of male supremacy which now is a central doctrine and ingrained practice in the party.

The party's capitulation to sex chauvinism has been a long-standing scandal in the SWP periphery, and that it has not been noticed and exposed by our opponents is only a commentary on the general backwardness of socialist thought in this country.

The party is now committed to its point-blank refusal to undertake the special indicated effort that would tap the enormous potential of revolutionary energy among oppressed and doubly-exploited women.

The central party leadership is essentially hostile to women leaders, as well as to anyone who considers Second Sexhood to be a political and organizational issue. Both the letter and spirit of Bolshevism on the question are alien to the SWP leadership.

VI. Youth

Indoctrinated in political sectarianism and organizational fetishism, the party youth, largely deprived of any workingclass background or experience, are further deprived by the party of a solid theoretical training, and they accordingly move ahead even faster than the older cadres on the road toward careerism, maneuverism, organizational manipulations, monolithic structure, and contempt for theory, history and principled politics.

Many of these young middleclass intellectuals could be inspired and educated to become worker-Bolsheviks. Instead, their pragmatism and cautiousness are fanned by the rigidity and conservatism of the central leadership.

As the younger comrades proceed to assume increasing

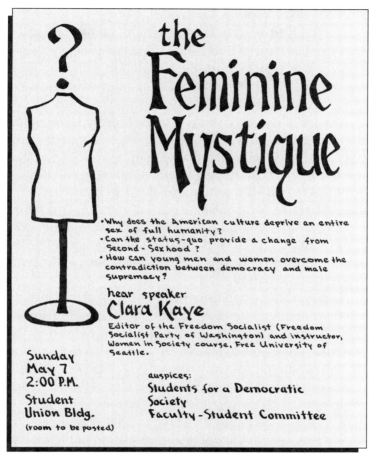

Leaflet for a mid-1960s forum sponsored by University of Washington SDS featuring FSP founder Clara Fraser (Kaye).

control of the party apparatus, the SWP will soon become as unrecognizable to others as it is to us today, for the youth are encouraged to exaggerate the very worst features of the party.

The best of the youth, those with a truly revolutionary ardor and understanding will not be able to survive in the stifling, narrow, and mechanistic confines of the party. The SWP is dooming the best of today's radical youth to disorientation and eventual demoralization.

VII. *The Organization Question*

For some 15 years—since Comrades Dobbs and Kerry organized the Seattle Cochranites for an unprincipled organizational assault against the local leadership—we have well realized the preeminence the majority attaches to organizational matters.

Nevertheless, we have persistently presented our *political* ideas to the party, entering into discussions wherever possible, but devoting the overwhelming bulk of our time and thought to year-in, year-out party building and branch activity. We helped organize branches for co-thinkers, kept the SWP on the local and national ballot, made Trotskyism a living reality with an unbroken tradition in the Pacific Northwest, and built what may well be the most consistently active and flourishing proletarian branch in the party over a 20-year period.

Armed with the traditions of the movement and seeking to preserve them, we made politics central and organizational questions secondary, refusing to be provoked by the constant attempt of the majority to undermine our position by organizational harassment, personal slander and intricate maneuverism. So long as the possibility of free exchange of views existed, we kept the doors open for discussion by minimizing all administrative and secondary assaults.

But precisely as the political degradation of the leadership accelerated, its intolerance of oppositional ideas intensified. Despite all our tremendous efforts, it has been impossible to obtain a climate of principled politics. Every political dispute and discussion is muddled and prejudiced by organizational smoke screen grievances, threats, frame-ups around "security" claims, blatant falsification of oppositional ideas and the incessant grinding-out of National Office-inspired corridor gossip.

Our tendency stood for proletarian democracy in the party, for the right of minority representation on leading bodies, and for a comradely exchange of ideas. The majority position is that the majority *is* the party and that a minority is inherently anti-party, dangerous, diseased and intolerable, and must be driven out. All opposition is treated factionally, and all factions are reduced to the status of outlaws.

The central leadership has become a peculiar anti-political clique which has consolidated its control of the apparatus by driving out all dissidents, critics, and potential critics within the leadership, engineered parallel purges in the ranks, and is now attaching itself to a predominantly petty-bourgeois student social base.

To answer critics, the majority refuses analytical argument and simply reiterates doctrine, thereby demonstrating that the SWP has become essentially a doctrinaire party without any internal ideological life in the full meaning of the term.

Trotskyism in the SWP image has become transformed into a graven image.

Loyalty to the leadership has assumed the proportions of cultism. The cult has taken form in the majority caucus, which now comprises virtually the entire SWP and is maintained for the sole purpose of preventing open discussion in the party. It merges comrades of many and varying political positions around the central issue of organizational loyalty to the regime. It is thus a totally unprincipled bloc.

The recent plenum displayed the ultimate absurdity of this clique operation. There was in the entire plenum only one openly dissenting voice—Kirk's. Yet the Political Committee found it necessary to eliminate one whole plenum session in order to substitute for it a—majority caucus! And all basic decisions were made there rather than at the plenum where Kirk was allowed to be present (so he could be censured!).

Such a ridiculous practice makes frank, open and honest discussion of differences patently impossible. But it flows clearly from the 1965 Organizational Resolution, which climaxed the party descent into shameless anti-Bolshevism on the question of party organization.

Future of the SWP

Is the SWP irretrievably decayed? Is the degenerative process irreversible?

We do not know. We wholeheartedly hope not. The long and honorable record compiled by the party of anticapitalist principle, plus the tremendous dynamism of the Trotsky heritage and the Cannon interventionism into the living struggle wherever it broke through, created a cadre with essentially workingclass and revolutionary reflexes. But these reflexes became paralyzed by the fetish of loyalty to the leadership and the concomitant horror of any criticism of the leadership.

In the future, some social force outside the party might jolt the majority enough to jar it out of its sublime complacency. But for now, the party will neither intervene publicly with ideology nor discuss objectively the unsolved problems of the American Revolution.

Our course

Considering the present insupportable circumstances, we cannot waste any more of our time and resources in trying to avoid the running organizational hunt-and-kill game which the majority imposes upon us as the price of our remaining in the party.

The plenum decision to censure Kirk for nonexistent "crimes" and then to investigate them, and the Political Committee announcement that the Seattle Branch's protest against and rejection of the censure was "inauthentic," anonymous and therefore unreal, telegraphs the determination of the PC to destroy the Seattle Branch and rid the party of any general critics of the leadership.

At a time when the Seattle Branch was preparing for the International Day of Protest, working in two local CEWVs [Committees to End the War in Vietnam], anticipating a northwest conference of the antiwar movement, involved in a northern trip which we were invited to make by co-thinkers, active in trying to cement a viable local African defense committee, planning a new forum series, etc., etc., etc.—it has been unceasingly barraged by the Center as the leadership escalates its deliberate sabotage of our daily party-building work.

Still, despite everything, under different conditions we might still try to remain in the party founded by Trotsky and developed by Cannon. *But the SWP is no longer the epicenter of revolutionary activity and ideology in the U.S.* Its estrangement from the Negro struggle and its refusal to intervene rationally and politically in the antiwar movement, or in the present rebirth of interest in socialist thought, have destroyed its chance, for this period, to secure ideological hegemony over the non-Stalinist Left—a necessary first step toward political hegemony over the class.

This opportunity was presented to the party by the 20th Congress and the following period of regroupment, rising colonial revolution, the Sino-Soviet conflict, and the international crisis of capitalism. But the leadership has squandered its capital and clearly announced that it is not interested in creating today the basis of the party of the American Revolution. That is always for mañana.

We hope to be able to intervene in the viable political currents all around us today. Outside the SWP, and without programmatic affinity for any other existing party, we may not be able to demonstrably prove the superiority of our policies. Yet we intend to intervene. Freed from the persecutory mania of the SWP, we will do what we can to further the principles of Trotskyism in those arenas where the SWP is unwilling or unable to intervene politically. Some Trotskyists must try to publicize and promote our rich heritage of thought, especially when so many doors in the mass movement today are swinging open, all over the country.

Summary

We have clear political differences with the regime on the questions of the Negro struggle, the colonial revolution, the Vietnamese war, regroupment, women's emancipation, and party organizational principles. We have a different appraisal of the import and nature of the present conjuncture, and a different strategical perspective on the unfolding of the American Revolution.

We do not consider these differences fundamentally incompatible with party membership.

The majority, however, so considers them, and will not let us live and function in the party we built.

The majority also exploits our very existence as a minority tendency to pressure everybody else into line. They thus force us to play the objective role of helping to cement the anti-democratic and anti-political leadership clique.

We therefore consider it our responsibility to resign our memberships in the SWP and put an end to the otherwise unending organizational farce played by the Center against its internal opponents, against the principles of the movement, and particularly against the needs and interests of the burgeoning radical movement in the U.S.

We are resigning in protest against the kind of a party the SWP has become. We are resigning because we see no realistic chance of being allowed to even criticize it.

We hope that some day the SWP will find its road cleared for the historic return to the method of Leninism in theory, program, tactics and party life.

[Signed by]

22 members of Seattle Branch SWP

3 Connecticut supporters of Kirk-Kaye Tendency

3 Seattle Non-SWP YSAers
who concurrently resigned from YSA
on the basis of this statement

Statement by the former Seattle Branch on SWP and YSA disruption
May 15, 1966

A host of political hatchet men from New York, California and Canada, dispatched at tremendous financial cost by the National Office of the Socialist Workers Party and Young Socialist Alliance, failed miserably in their blitzkrieg attempt to disrupt and demoralize a conference of socialist youth held here on April 24th for the purpose of probing the possibilities of forming a new independent revolutionary youth organization.

This latest YSA super-factional outrage occurred shortly after the Seattle Branch of the SWP and the Seattle YSA resigned from their national organizations.

No fewer than nine imports were sent to Seattle in an hysterical revenge reaction aimed at smashing the now-independent Seattle Trotskyists. The national delegation included Tom Leonard of the New York SWP, Kipp Dawson of the California YSA, and John Britton of the National Office, YSA.

This nine-man shock troop attempted to throw the conference into chaos by challenging every point of business. They continually demanded the floor, heckled the presidium, caucused openly in the middle of the proceedings, and kept up a running harangue on the theme that "politics is bunk," that talking about revolution and Marxism today is ridiculous, and that the only task of radical youth was to get out into the streets and stop the war in Vietnam. Anyone interested in politics, they announced, might join the YSA— but no other political organization! They pressed their "single-issue" concept of the antiwar struggle in a manner not seen locally since the days of Stalinist domination of the radical movement.

The unfortunate political and tactical degeneration of the SWP and YSA have now been blatantly exposed to the entire antiwar and leftwing movement in Seattle. It should be clear to all that these organizations are marred by conservative hostility towards any development not directly under their control; their attitude toward all other formations moving in a revolutionary direction is rigidly sectarian and assumes the organizational form of all-out disruption.

The "crime" of the local revolutionary youth was that they were setting up a genuinely independent and autonomous organization based upon a clear revolutionary program.

This latest SWP scandal in Seattle was only the climax of a two-week campaign of disruption, begun at the Northwest Conference Against the War in Vietnam held here in April. An official representative of the *Militant*, Asher Harer from San Francisco, launched a vicious attack from the floor of this conference against Larry Shumm, a local spokesman of the YSA (who has since resigned) who was one of a panel of five speakers on the subject of "Political Action for the Antiwar Movement." Harer was indignant at Shumm's expression of revolutionary solidarity with the National Liberation Front in Vietnam.[82] In an incredible display of opportunism and demagogy, Harer cried, "Shumm is telling the mothers of American GIs dying in Vietnam that their sons should be driven into the sea and drowned!"

Harer announced that national SWP policy was not being followed by the then Seattle Branch, and he informed the audience that the Northwest antiwar movement was a very bad movement and doomed to defeat unless it followed the line of the SWP to keep out of politics. Talk of socialism, he said, amounted to scabbery in the middle of a strike.

The audience was stunned and disgusted at this public display of internal SWP disputes. The chairman immediately recognized Dick Fraser, a leader of the Seattle Branch, who apologized to the conference for the disruption, condemned Harer's anti-politicalism in a panel devoted to the examination of what political road was indicated for the movement, and went on to advocate an anti-capitalist electoral coalition in the state of Washington for the coming elections.

SWP and YSA have to date colonized approximately six people (we do not know the exact number) in Seattle whose proclaimed purpose is to wage war on the former Seattle Branch. Their approach and tactics are those of any ruthless trade union machine intent on obliterating an opposition. They are undertaking a political scorched path policy and their methods have inevitably boomeranged against them.

They have solidified the indigenous and knowledgeable radical movement against them, discredited themselves among the radical youth, and are held responsible for a scandalous outrage against the antiwar united front and against principled politics.

The youth conference on April 24th heard out and debated with the invading SWP and YSA delegations, invited them to leave if they opposed the purpose of the gathering, watched them walk out, and then proceeded to organize towards a new revolutionary socialist local youth movement.

Some radicals in this area questioned the reports of horrifying SWP and YSA behavior at the Thanksgiving NCC [National Coordinating Committee to End the War in Vietnam] conference in Washington, DC, and were willing to give those organizations the benefit of the doubt. That reasonable doubt has now been categorically resolved; SWP and YSA are being seen in action right here in Seattle, and contemptible new stains are being added to the once-proud banners of those two organizations.

The huge financial expense of transporting and subsidizing an entire group of full-time organizers in Seattle—hardly a key political center of the country!—is being borne by SWP and YSA out of purely factional motives. At a time when the concept of the united front and fraternal relations among radical organizations is being steadily transformed into reality, SWP and YSA alone continue to act on a course of utterly bureaucratic and sectarian tactics. We deplore the terrible political and organizational ossification of what was once the party of Leon Trotsky.

Why we left the Socialist Workers Party
Public statement by
Richard Kirk, Clara Kaye, Frank Krasnowsky,
David Dreiser and Waymon Ware

On behalf of the former Seattle Branch of the Socialist Workers Party, and other SWPers who supported the Marxist evaluation of the Negro Question developed by Richard Kirk, we present this statement explaining why we left the SWP—that party to which most of us have devoted our entire lives since our youth.

Origin of the Kirk-Kaye tendency

Our political group, known within the SWP as the Kirk-Kaye tendency, was formalized at the 1957 convention of the party, when we opposed the unprincipled adaptation of the SWP to the pacifist-reformist leadership of the Negro struggle. Adulation of Dr. King replaced a revolutionary approach to the question within the party, and heralded a process of degeneration which reached a decisive stage at the 1963 national convention of the party.

In that year, the SWP proclaimed a boycott of the Southern struggle, condemned leftward-moving SNCC as "reformist/integrationist," and turned toward Elijah Muhammad and the Black Muslims as the "most dynamic" section of the Negro movement.

In regard to other areas of the class struggle, the 1963 convention rejected the perspective of socialist regroupment and deepened its hostility towards all the new leftward moving organizations on the political scene; the perspective of political revolution in China was reaffirmed; party organizational procedures were formally "tightened up" while an ongoing purge of critics of the leadership was accelerated.

Our tendency opposed this course. We particularly resisted the slanderous identification of the southern militants with "tokenism," and the all-out support of Negro separatism.

Our counter-resolution to the convention, "Revolutionary Integration," called on the SWP to permit its Negro cadre to intervene in the living struggle for equality with a Marxist program. We developed our thesis that the Negro movement for equality is a unique and central phenomenon of the class struggle in the United States, integrally connected with the proletarian struggle for socialism.

The SWP espouses "Black separatism"

The SWP leadership rejected the interconnection of the Freedom Now and socialist movements. The ease with which the SWP slid over from adaptation to Rev. King to glorification of Mr. Muhammad expressed the basically false theory—inherited from the Communist Party—that the Negro Question in the U.S. is only a variation of the National Question in Eastern Europe.

This theory maintains that the Negro problem can be solved by "self-determination" and racial separation. Thus, all policy problems of the Negro movement can be solved without strenuous analysis and thought, for the SWP leadership says in effect that whatever the Negro leadership does is good enough for the Negroes and good enough for the SWP because whatever policy is most prominent at any stage has been "self-determined."

The SWP's confusion of the *mood of Black nationalism* with the *politics of separatism* bore bitter fruit when Malcolm X engineered a split in the Black Muslims. Malcolm was clearly oriented toward combining the ghetto struggle with the southern movement and with socialism. He denounced the Muslims for their basically reactionary character, and consequently felt the wrath of Mr. Muhammad's goons. The SWP, supporting Muslim unity, was caught in its own trap. It became both the supporter of Malcolm and the defender of his enemy and probable murderer.

The SWP, now discredited in the Negro community,

presents the ludicrous spectacle of an all-white party with a Black nationalist program.

Our perspective on the unfolding American Revolution

The logic of the SWP's position on the Negro struggle led to a de facto isolation of the party from the struggle, for Black nationalism itself stands aside from the main thrust of the Negro struggle—the fight against segregation. We now felt impelled to publish within the party an analysis of the basic reasons for the party's sectarianism on this and other vital questions.

Since 1957, we had responded to severe changes occurring in the party program by formulating our own position on a number of domestic and international issues. We believed that the party was departing from the dynamic course dictated by the spirit and letter of Leninism and Trotskyism, and that it was stagnating into conservatism.

In what proved to be a vain effort to arrest this general drift, we submitted to the national 1965 convention an extensive Political Resolution dealing with the current stage of the crisis of U.S. imperialism and the consequent strategy and tactics needed for the realization of our revolution. We sought to orient the party toward the Negro struggle as the crux of the American Revolution, and toward China as the key to the colonial revolution and the major policy problem of the international revolutionary movement. The resolution also called attention to the essentially anti-capitalist nature of the struggle of women and youth today, and concluded that the road to the American Revolution did not lie directly through the trade union movement, but followed the course of the struggles of the most oppressed wherever they broke out. We said it was the destiny of these struggles outside the labor movement to become the vitalizing currents that would eventually move the labor movement and become the vanguard of the revolutionary movement as a whole.

We called for a commitment to the struggles of women under capitalism, and for the formation of a truly independent revolutionary youth movement.

The SWP becomes monolithic

The convention rejected our perspective and tactics. Indeed, rank-and-file consideration of our resolution was virtually impossible as the long-honored internal democracy of the party had by then been destroyed by a protracted "tightening up" campaign. The majority was hostile to all criticism and any new proposals emanating from outside the leadership. The proletarian principle of minority representation on all leading bodies was abandoned and the very right of factions to exist was denied in a new Organizational Resolution submitted by the leadership and adopted by the convention.

The majority simply refused to debate the issues in dispute and discussion was effectively proscribed. Instead, we were threatened and denounced over local administrative practices. This type of unprincipled politics was fast becoming characteristic of the party leadership.

We concluded from this experience that the SWP had become a doctrinaire party, mired in a "holding operation," i.e., a prolonged state of suspension based on the assumption that nothing significant can happen until the revival of the trade unions and the emergence of a labor party. The SWP was ossifying around conjunctural evaluations of 25 years ago, and neither changes in national or world conditions, the isolation and disasters resulting from its own mistakes, nor the loss of its basic cadre of revolutionary Negroes, women, unionists and intellectuals could shake its complacency.

The last struggle—over antiwar policy

The policy of the SWP leadership in the antiwar movement brought our differences to the breaking point.

After standing aside from the antiwar movement during its critical formative stages, the SWP decided in mid-1965 to plunge in—for an organizational raid.

We made one last attempt to prevent a disaster for Trotskyism in the U.S.

We protested against the single-issue, anti-political policy of SWP and YSA which led them into the presumptuous demand that the Thanksgiving NCC [National Coordinating Committee to End the War in Vietnam] conference in Washington, D.C. center its deliberations around the party's peculiar and confusing organizational proposals, rather than around questions of program and principle. This course was unprecedented in our movement. We denied the SWP characterization of the left wing of the antiwar movement as "Stalinist." We condemned their fearful refusal to proclaim clear support to the National Liberation Front and their super-cautious and outdated policy on the draft, which prevents effective opposition to it.

We advocated a proletarian antiwar policy that would solidarize the party with the revolution in Vietnam, with workingclass Negro youth who are the key victims of the draft, and with the radical wing of the antiwar movement.

The SWP substitutes organizational attacks for political debate

The party's policy in the antiwar movement had never been subject to rank-and-file discussion. Comrade Kirk, a member of the National Committee for 25 years, requested a debate on the issue within the National Committee. He flew to New York to participate in it, and discovered that the chief results of his protest were punitive organizational measures directed against him personally, against the Seattle Branch as a whole, and against other supporters of the tendency. Such measures are understood within the party to be a prelude to expulsion.

Under such circumstances, the resignation we had contemplated for some time became inevitable.

The SWP's estrangement from the Negro struggle and its refusal to intervene politically in the antiwar movement or in the present rebirth of interest in socialist thought have removed it for this period from the epicenter of revolutionary activity and ideology in the U.S. We would welcome a turn which would reverse this tragic degenerative process, but we cannot wait for this possibility. There are more vital things to do in the class struggle than conduct a futile and debilitating internecine organizational struggle over tertiary administrative issues. Since every political difference and discussion is now muddied and prejudiced by an organizational smoke screen thrown over it by the party leadership to obscure the principled issues in dispute, the party can no longer contain critics. And revolutionaries who are not critical cannot maintain for long their revolutionary quality.

Our objectives

In resigning, we reaffirm our commitment to Marxism, to Leninism and to Trotskyism, and we have set forth these immediate objectives:

1) To join with other independent socialists in the Pacific Northwest in the creation of a new revolutionary socialist party here;

2) To continue collaboration with our colleagues throughout the country, with the object of making our views known to the various components within U.S. radicalism;

3) To advocate, support and participate in a revival and regeneration of Marxism in the U.S., and in a fundamental reorganization of socialists in a new revolutionary socialist party, able to unite the Negro vanguard with the socialist radicals. We believe this to be the indispensable formula for the foundation of a genuine revolutionary socialism in this country.

Our program

The following is the gist of the program we have developed and fought for within the SWP for many years. We are presenting it now publicly for the first time for the consideration of all revolutionary socialists and all mass movement militants and radicals.

I. For a revolutionary Marxist approach to the Negro struggle

The connection between the proletarian struggle for socialism and the Negro struggle for equality is *integral* and proclaims the unfolding of the Permanent Revolution in the U.S.

The fascist-like police states of the South are structurally basic to the capitalist political economy of the U.S. The struggle against segregation, therefore, threatens the entire nationwide social system. This fact demonstrates the impossibility of achieving equality under U.S. capitalism, and it further transforms the demand for integration into a transitional revolutionary demand. This in turn guarantees the emergence of a revolutionary left wing that will contend for leadership against the reformist/tokenists in the civil rights movement.

The development of all-Black organizations expresses and cultivates the pride and self-reliance of the most oppressed, and opens new avenues in the struggle for freedom. But these so-called "nationalist" formations do not result from any inherent drive toward national separatism, but from organizational needs and from an internationalism that identifies the Negro struggle with the colonial revolution. The demands of the essentially proletarian masses express the historic needs of the working class as a whole in the struggle against capitalist exploitation.

No amount of all-Black independence can overcome the terrible isolation of the Negro masses from the white working class and the socialist movement. What is revealed here is the backwardness of the labor movement and the theoretical bankruptcy of the established Left. This isolation is a mortal danger both to the freedom struggle and to the struggle for socialism, since each is impossible without the other.

The Negro struggle is the central question of the American Revolution and the Negro movement is the vanguard sector of the entire working class. That is why the Negro movement is the first target of reaction: racism and the southern system are the launching pads of American fascism.

The Negro movement must be encouraged to develop a Marxist program and cadre that can unite the ghetto masses with the southern struggle into a powerful revolutionary force, and there can then be forged a working alliance among the Negro vanguard, socialist revolutionaries and the militants in the white working class.

This is the key to the American Revolution.

II. For solidarity with the Chinese Revolution

The Chinese Revolution upset the international class peace agreed to at Potsdam and Teheran. This great revolution confirmed once again the validity of Trotsky's thesis of Permanent Revolution by demonstrating that the national revolution in backward countries cannot achieve its goals of national independence, national unification and economic growth without going over to the stage of socialist revolution.

China's experience (not lost on the Cuban revolutionaries) established China as the key to the colonial revolution and the principal target of world imperialism.

At first in practice, and then in an ideological polemic against the Soviet bureaucracy, the Chinese CP opposed the policy of class collaboration with world imperialism as expounded and practiced by both Stalin and the current Soviet leadership. The international debate which ensued, forcing world Communism to examine the issues, began the creation of revolutionary tendencies who opposed the reformist leaderships throughout the Communist movement. The necessary prerequisites were thereby established for an international revolutionary regroupment.

Still, the progressive character of the international role of the Communist Party of China is severely limited by the residue of Stalinism. The Khrushchev revelations about Stalin at the 20th Congress of the Communist Party of the Soviet Union revealed the cracks in the Soviet bureaucracy which might have been exploited by the Soviet workers to the point of political revolution against the entire regime and the reinstitution of proletarian democracy in the Soviet Union. But the Chinese Communist Party by its public adulation of Stalin and Stalinism struck a severe blow at the democratic aspirations of the Soviet proletariat and thus helped to re-cement the power of the bureaucratic caste in the Soviet Union.

The Chinese Communist Party stubbornly maintains Mao's theory—not fundamentally different from Stalin's—that the national revolution in colonial countries can be carried to fruition by a joint dictatorship of the proletariat and the native bourgeoisie—in spite of the Chinese party's own experience which refutes this theory!

The disastrous results of the policy flowing from this theory are to be seen in Indonesia. The Chinese leadership must share responsibility for the policy followed by the Indonesian Communist movement, a policy in no way distinguishable from that of the CP in China in the '20s in respect to the Kuomintang and Chiang Kai-shek, and a policy that produced the identical end: massacre and utter rout.

The Chinese Communist Party's favorable references to Stalin result from this chronic contradiction in both their theory and practice.

China's internal life, however, differs sharply from the Soviet model. Clearly absent is the immense privileged bureaucracy, wielding arbitrary authority through an all-powerful secret police. The concentration camps and blood purges that are the hallmarks of Stalinism are also absent. The expanding role of the workers and peasants in economic planning and control, have resulted in a consistent economic growth and a realistic potential for greater proletarian democracy.

The Chinese Communists are sensitive to the growth of bureaucracy in China. But they cannot ultimately prevent its growth so long as they remain blind to its origin and history in the USSR. While the very symbol of bureaucratic privilege and tyranny—Stalin—continues to be idolized in China, they will hover on the verge of retrogression and degeneration.

Likewise, their Stalinist heritage prevents the Chinese CP from playing a decisive role in the reorganization of a worldwide revolutionary international.

III. For serious politics in the antiwar movement

The capitalist class has a fundamental stake in the war in Vietnam and will not withdraw short of a military/political defeat or virtual civil war at home. The only way that the American people can stop this war is through a mass political movement of the working class.

Vanguard elements of the antiwar movement feel their isolation from the working class to be a basic weakness of the movement; they seek alliances with the proletariat and specifically with the Negroes, that section of the working class already in motion. As a consequence of a serious effort to stop the war, antiwar militants are groping for fundamental solutions to social problems. They seek to unite Negroes, the poverty-stricken, draft resisters, radical unionists, socialists, etc., into a broad political movement.

Revolutionary Marxists should help them find the correct road to political unity by demonstrating the necessity of independent anti-capitalist politics that connect the war to the other evils of the system. Political ventures short of such a program are doomed to eventual capitulation to the Democratic Party and other forms of class collaboration politics.

The liberal plea for "negotiations" with the Vietnamese Revolution must be exposed; the only principled slogan is "Withdraw U.S. Troops Now." But when the demand for withdrawal is devoid of a meaningful economic analysis of the cause of war, even this slogan fosters the illusion that the antiwar movement by itself will pressure the U.S. out of Vietnam. The notion that simply more activism and more protesters can end the war is an essentially pacifist proposition. This unrealistic and anti-political approach is a dangerous conservative barrier to the political development of the antiwar movement.

IV. For a revolutionary approach to the Woman Question

We place the struggle for women's emancipation on the level of a first-class theoretical and programmatic question.

As the first tendency in the history of American radicalism to formally incorporate this question into our basic program, we proclaim our resistance to the creeping paralysis of male supremacy which by now has become an ingrained practice in the entire labor and socialist movement, and a growing danger in the civil rights movement.

The leading role of women in the fight for civil rights, in the antiwar movement, in civil liberties campaigns, etc., is not accidental, but results from the special dynamic developed by women as an oppressed sex, seeking liberation for themselves and for all other victims of discrimination.

The feminine mystique, along with racism, remains the Achilles heel of the labor movement and a significant factor in the history of union degeneration. Women's equality must be raised as a transitional slogan whose dynamism flows from the pivotal location of the Woman Question in U.S. life, where the oppression and special exploitation of women is a burning injustice that intersects with every other political question and social movement.

V. For revolutionary unification and the
regeneration of socialist thought

Conditions for a meaningful discussion of Marxist ideology and for the creation of a united revolutionary socialist party have rarely been as favorable as they are today.

The essentially anti-capitalist character of the Freedom Now and antiwar movements draws the militants from both movements together in a search for political unity.

The end of the Stalin era and the current Sino-Soviet dispute have weakened old prejudices and created an atmosphere favoring political discussion in the socialist movement. The crisis of capitalism, demonstrated by the permanent war policy of the Democratic administration and its hypocrisy in civil rights and anti-poverty, has forced onetime liberals and pacifists into a serious consideration of Marxism. An entire generation of radical youth, disgusted by its inheritance, and enthused by the courage and determination of the colonial revolutionists abroad and the freedom fighters at home, is seeking more effective methods and ideas for the struggle against capitalism.

Revolutionary Marxists must accelerate and help give form to this growing need for a new socialist movement. We must add to the energy, inventiveness, and boldness of the New Left the most important qualities of the Trotskyist Old Left: Marxist ideology, a proletarian orientation, experience in the class struggle, and the recognition of the need for a centralized, disciplined and thoroughly democratic revolutionary party.

Why we organized a new socialist party

From a statement distributed to reporters at the first press conference of the Freedom Socialist Party,
July 1966, Seattle, Washington

We represent revolutionary socialists from nearly all the existing socialist parties.

Some of us represent the former Seattle branches of the Socialist Workers Party and the Young Socialist Alliance, which broke away from their national organizations because of serious programmatic differences surrounding the nature of the Negro struggle, antiwar policy, woman's emancipation and the strategical perspectives of the American revolution.

Some of us represent the militant tendency of the old Communist Party, a group which left the CP many years ago after it became clear that the CP had ceased to operate upon genuine revolutionary principles and tactics, and merely sought to reform the existing social system. In the interests of "peaceful coexistence," the CP actually succeeds only in preserving the status quo.

Some of us represent the new generation of radical youth who are sincerely pressing for a fundamental social change and who are contemptuous of the so-called "radical" organizations which are predominantly concerned with creating an image of respectability. These organizations actually prevent real solutions insofar as they join the reformists in working within the Democratic Party. Some of our younger members are former adherents of the Socialist Party of Norman Thomas, which has gone over to the Democrats completely.

We are a party of militant and radical trade unionists, youth, Negroes, women, pensioners, students and professionals who believe in a new social system and a new way of life for the United States.

■   ■   ■

We are attempting to express the need in this country for a vast reorganization and regroupment of the radical movement upon a principled program of revolutionary socialism and internal democracy.

Millions of Americans are becoming conscious today of the desperate need for basic social change. The Black Power movement, the antiwar movement, the restless stirrings inside the labor movement—all reveal the need and can create the foundation for a dynamic and broadly based new socialist movement.

■   ■   ■

We are distinguished from all other socialist trends by the following programmatic characteristics:

(1) We are for regroupment of the revolutionary socialist movement and for a regeneration of socialist theory and thought. These issues are interconnected.

Any real reorganization is impossible without an ideological confrontation between the various revolutionary socialist tendencies and a probing for areas of agreement and dissent. To achieve this meaningful theoretical confrontation, all extant parties will need to learn to overcome their sectarian hostility to each other on secondary and organizational matters. Proclamations of a self-ordained exclusive revolutionary franchise, and unproven condemnations of opponents as "counterrevolutionary" only serve to atomize the radical movement and prevent the joint elaboration of Marxist theory into a guide to action.

It is *program* that must delineate differences and similarities, and simultaneously stimulate united fronts for joint action.

The central problem flows from the isolation of Marxists from the American working class, and from theoretical-political failure to comprehend both the dynamic of international revolutionary developments and the nature of the unfolding revolution in the United States. Socialists in this country have always demonstrated an unwholesome attachment to pragmatism, and the first step for any revolutionary regroupment must be the revival of *Marxist theory as a guide to action.*

Marxist theory must be grasped and seriously applied to perspectives of the American revolution and to conjunctural analyses. Socialist and radical currents and individuals who consider themselves revolutionary must engage in a national dialog and debate over the THEORY of the American revolution. Out of this honest and serious discussion can emerge a reorganization of the socialist vanguard, realistically geared to effective intervention into the coming mass radicalization.

(2) We believe that the Negro freedom movement is a unique and central phenomenon of the class struggle in the U.S., integrally connected with the proletarian struggle for socialism. Black freedom fighters are the vanguard sector of the entire working class; their development into full-fledged social revolutionaries is the key to the emergence of a revolutionary socialist leadership in this country.

We call for a Second Reconstruction in the South. The southern states should be declared illegal because of their inability to provide a republican form of government as guaranteed by the Constitution. We call for new regimes, elected by universal suffrage and maintained by a Peoples Militia.

(3) We advocate to the antiwar movement the truth that only fundamental social change can end the war in Vietnam and the constant escalation of U.S. aggression against the colonial revolution.

The capitalist class and the government it controls consider Vietnam central to its basic aim of ruling the world and defending U.S. economic interests. The U.S. will not withdraw from this conflict unless it is militarily defeated by the National Liberation Front of Vietnam or stalemated by paralyzing social crisis at home. Such a crisis can be precipitated by the intervention of the U.S. working class into the field

155

of foreign policy by means of the general strike, or by the threatening power of a new independent and anti-capitalist political party with mass support. New upsurges in the world revolution will certainly affect the Pentagon's military timetable in Vietnam, but the decisive ending of the war will result only from a revolutionary new political conjuncture in U.S. politics.

(4) We are for the elevation of the Woman Question—the fact of the secondary economic, social, political, legal and psychological status of women in the U.S.—to a first-rank programmatic issue for socialists.

(5) We are for alerting the working class and the socialist vanguard to a more serious awareness of the imminent danger of fascism in this country and a more profound understanding of its character.

U.S. capital must turn to fascism as the only means of maintaining political and economic equilibrium. The one-man dictatorial rule in the White House, the present solidarity between northern fascist trends and the southern KKK, and the growing consolidation of the neo-fascist movements, are all signs of the mounting inability of capitalism to continue to rule through the democratic process. The ideological and political climate is being prepared for a fascist takeover in the coming crisis.

■   ■   ■

Bold new elements in the Black Power movement, in the antiwar movement, and in the general New Left are groping for fundamental solutions, seeking to find a way to unite all radicals prepared to follow the struggle through to the end. The new radicals are seeking a connection with the broad proletariat—the decisive class in our revolution. This ongoing radicalization can culminate in the creation of a mature revolutionary combat party, a party that will proclaim its readiness to assume responsibility for the American revolution.

The Freedom Socialist Party calls on all revolutionaries

to join with us and help us try to give form to this intensifying need for a new socialist movement. We must add to the energy, inventiveness, and defiance of the New Left the most important qualities of the Trotskyist Old Left: Marxist theory, a proletarian orientation, experience in the class struggle, and the recognition of the functional necessity for a centralized, disciplined and thoroughly democratic revolutionary party.

Program of the FSP
Adopted at the FSP Founding Conference, July 1966

Preamble

Both the needs and the opportunity exist in the U.S. today for a fundamental reorganization, regroupment and coalescence of socialist vanguard elements into a new revolutionary socialist movement.

As the post-World War II economic boom draws to a close, a deep crisis is rapidly maturing for U.S. imperialism. This crisis is already engendering the objective and human forces for social rebellion and a new political movement.

1. The 20-year-long economic upsurge has been powered by the need to replace the fixed capital destroyed by the previous 15 years of depression and war (1929-1944). The lack of new opportunities for capital investment is now threatening to terminate capitalist expansion, forcing the U.S. into desperate aggression to solidify spheres of investment.

The war in Vietnam expresses this stage of the general crisis of capitalism and is part of a series of barbarous wars against the colonial world.

2. Meanwhile, the *colonial revolution* itself has advanced to a new stage.

The first waves of the postwar revolution in colonial countries placed the native capitalist class in power. Ten years were sufficient to demonstrate that capitalism could no longer provide an economic framework for developing nations, and today in Asia, Latin America and Africa, it is becoming crystal clear that the socialist alternative is the only solution to the chronic crisis of underdeveloped lands.

The current *proletarian stage* of the colonial revolution, begun in China and continued in Cuba, constantly threatens to detach more strategic politico-economic sectors from the area of imperialist exploitation.

3. As political and military crises accumulate in the international arena, *the Negro revolt* continues to create vast turmoil in U.S. politics, revealing its capability of paralyzing the government and inspiring sympathetic demonstrations of a revolutionary nature here and abroad.

4. A new generation, first moved to public expression of resistance to the status quo by the student anti-segregation movement of the South, is now in the forefront of a broad anti-war movement which comprises important sections of the old pacifist movement, the new-founded student radical organizations, and widening sectors of the civil rights movement.

■ ■ ■

The incipient economic crisis, the new stage of the colonial revolution, the velocity of the Negro revolt, and the growing sentiment against the war are all symptoms of the crisis of U.S. and world capitalism.

These factors indicate the chronic antagonism between reaction and socialism, and point toward a coming international showdown between imperialism and the social revolution.

I. For world socialism

(1) For genuine internationalism

The socialist revolution is worldwide and unified in character, although distinct from nation to nation in time and national peculiarities. The working class is essentially an international class with identical interests the world over. Any concession, therefore, to bourgeois nationalism in any country, is a blow to the international solidarity of the oppressed.

The idea that the interests of the working class and peasantry of any country may be sacrificed for the benefit of a given workers state is foreign to genuine internationalism. This reactionary doctrine, expressed in the theory of "socialism in one country" as developed in the USSR, must be identified, exposed and resisted by all revolutionaries.

(2) Defend the colonial revolution by promoting our revolution

Since the defeat of the European socialist and communist mass movements of the '30s, and particularly since their default during the post-World War II revolutionary opportunities, the center of gravity of world revolution has temporarily shifted to the colonial sector.

We defend the colonial revolution unconditionally against the assault of imperialism, recognizing that only the overthrow of capitalism and the establishment of workers states can bring about real political independence and economic growth.

Yet all revolutions are held in jeopardy until the ruling capitalist class in the industrial centers—and particularly in the U.S.—is displaced by proletarian power. Revolutions in the industrial centers are decisive for the ultimate victory of socialism anywhere.

(3) For socialist democracy

The new workers states that came into existence outside the Soviet bloc were beset by the problems of industrial backwardness, political isolation, and imperialist encirclement. These conditions made it necessary for them to develop a powerful centralization in order to attain both economic growth and a viable defense against bourgeois opposition from within and from the external world.

Yet this necessity does not contradict the corollary necessity for the expansion of workers democracy. On the contrary, it is all the more required! Only workingclass control of all the institutions of the revolution, exercised through formal bodies like soviets or communes, can curb the trend to bureaucratism, resist bourgeois pressures, and deepen the economic, political and cultural gains of the revolution.

In the Soviet Union, due to long isolation and extreme economic and cultural backwardness, a bureaucratic caste emerged in the '20s, based on the more privileged layers of the population. This bureaucracy was able to overthrow the original Bolshevik leadership of the Russian Revolution and consolidate its power. Today, this reactionary formation is vast and deeply entrenched, subject to removal only by a political revolution that will restore the working class to power and resurrect the workers democracy of the early 1920s.

But as the revolutions in China and Cuba have revealed, Soviet-style bureaucratism is not an inevitable product of a revolution in a backward country. Such bureaucratism can be avoided precisely to the extent that it is consciously re-sisted in theory and practice, and the question of socialist development related ideologically to the long-overdue world revolution instead of to the utopian and self-defeating goal of "socialism in one country."

(4) Defend the Chinese Revolution

Now is the hour of great need of the Chinese Revolution for aid, the time for the defenders of the Chinese workers state to distinguish themselves by a *policy of defense*.

The Chinese revolution has not only been the key stimu-lus to the colonial revolution, but has presented an historic challenge to the Kremlin's international class collaboration. The Chinese revolutionary leadership has been thrust into the role of a new polarizing center for the world communist movement. Imperialism has accordingly chosen China as its main target for political and military attack.

The Chinese Communist Party still retains a holdover of Stalinist theory and program, and to resist bureaucratic growth and avoid such disasters as occurred in Indonesia, the Chinese Communist Party will need to overcome the contradiction in its ideology and advance to a consistent concept of the colonial revolution, internationalism, and socialist democracy. Only then can it lead in the reorganization of a worldwide revolutionary international.

II. For socialism in the United States

(1) For a complete and basic social change

The ills of capitalist society cannot be cured by reform. The capitalist class must be removed from political power and the means of production and distribution nationalized. This will create the economic foundation for a society based upon planned production for use instead of capitalist production for profit.

Collective ownership of the means of production under workers' control is the only solution to the present crisis of mankind.

(2) For immediate and unconditional economic, political and social equality for Negroes. An end to racism forever.

Forced racial segregation is fundamental to the capitalist political economy of the U.S., and the fascist-like police states of the South are structurally basic to the nationwide socio-economic system. The struggle against segregation, therefore, threatens the entire system, and is integrally connected with the proletarian struggle for socialism. That is why the movement for Black freedom is the first target of reaction, and that is why the southern system and racism are the launching pads of U.S. fascism.

It is impossible to achieve racial justice through reforms, since the demand for freedom is transformed by objective reality into a transitional revolutionary demand. The Negro movement thus manifests the unfolding of the Permanent Revolution in the United States.

As a special and unique movement, connected to but simultaneously distinct from the workingclass struggle for socialism, the movement requires and is developing its own organizations and its own leadership. An initial stage in this process is the formation of all-Black organizations which express and cultivate the pride and self-reliance of the most oppressed. But these so-called "nationalist" trends do not result from any inherent drive toward *national separatism*, but from *the needs of the struggle* and from an *internationalism* that identifies the Negro movement with the colonial revolution.

No amount of all-Black independence can overcome the terrible isolation of the Negro masses from the white working class and the socialist movement. This isolation reveals the backwardness of the labor movement and the theoretical bankruptcy of the established Left, and comprises a mortal danger to both the freedom movement and the struggle for socialism—since neither can win without the other.

The Negro struggle is the central question of the American revolution and the Negro movement is the vanguard sector of the class struggle. The movement, therefore, must be encouraged to develop a program and a cadre to contend against the reformist and tokenist leaders tied to the capitalist system. Only a revolutionary leadership can unite the ghetto masses with the southern struggle into a powerful revolutionary force, a force capable of forging a working alliance among the Negro vanguard, socialist revolutionaries, and white workingclass militants.

The emergence of a Negro Marxist cadre in the movement is clearly the key to the American revolution.

(3) Towards the proletariat

Marx explained that all social progress since the advent of class society and the civil state has been the result of the class struggle. Flowing from this, among the social classes of modern society, only the working class will in the final analysis be able to achieve a socialist transformation.

The present corrupted condition of labor unions and of many skilled and privileged workers does not render this historical truth obsolete.

The road to the American revolution does not lead directly through, or start out with, the trade union movement. Instead, the road follows the course of the struggles of the most oppressed wherever they break out. It is the destiny of the Negro struggle, of the antiwar movement, of the surge for women's rights, and of other sectors outside the labor movement to become the vitalizing currents that eventually will move the labor movement itself. The Negro leadership will become the vanguard of the revolutionary movement as a whole, and we will witness northern workers starting to mobilize against speedup, unemployment, astronomical taxation, inflation, injustice, fascism and war.

(4) Prepare the struggle against fascism

U.S. capitalism must destroy all democratic institutions and turn to fascism as the only means of maintaining political and economic equilibrium in the final crisis.

Symptoms of this danger abound: the attacks on civil liberties and the union movement, the national consolidation of the fascist movement and the ultra-right during the Goldwater campaign (1964), the unprecedented solidarity between northern fascist trends and the Klan, etc. A growing fascist movement feeds upon the actions of repressive governmental and state institutions (the police, CIA, FBI, HUAC, the military caste) and is nourished by the anti-Communist syndrome and the ideologies of white supremacy and male chauvinism.

The bypassing of Congress and the concentration of all vital political and economic decisions in the hands of the administration has made one-man dictatorial rule the norm. This "Bonapartism" is a prelude to fascism and paves the way for a violent takeover.

The working class must be alerted to this menace. Workers must insist upon the independence of their organizations from the capitalist structure and commit themselves uncompromisingly to the struggle for civil liberties and Black freedom. Workers must mobilize against fascist organizations as they appear.

(5) For independent political action

The injustice of society cannot be resolved by reforming capitalism, and the Democratic and Republican parties, created for the protection and maintenance of capitalism, can never be vehicles for more than token social progress.

Liberals or "radicals" who provide window dressing for the reactionary political machines, especially under the demagogic guise of "connecting with the masses" and "being realistic" paralyze these very masses and serve as obstacles to the necessary break with the twin parties of big business.

(6) For a revolutionary approach to the Woman Question

As the first tendency in the history of U.S. radicalism to formally incorporate this question into our basic program, we proclaim our resistance to the insidious doctrine of male supremacy which has become ingrained in U.S. culture, resulting in the paralysis of the labor and socialist movements and in a growing danger within the civil rights movement.

The special dynamic developed in women because of their special oppression as a sex must be encouraged and defended, while the feminine mystique must be exposed. Women's equality is a transitional slogan, its momentum flowing from the pivotal position of the Woman Question in U.S. life, where her oppression and peculiar exploitation is a burning injustice that intersects with every other political issue and social movement.

(7) For a proletarian antiwar policy

The united front for limited specific demands is the proper form for the broad movement against the war. But

This Cuban poster vividly depicts the connection between women's oppression and U.S. military aggression in Vietnam—a connection rarely made by the U.S. Left except by the Freedom Socialist Party.

the duty of socialists is to go further and tell the truth about this war with the object of raising the political understanding of the movement and mobilizing it for political action.

The liberal plea for "Negotiations" with the Vietnamese Revolution must be exposed: the only principled slogan is "Withdraw U.S. Troops Now." But a demand for withdrawal that is devoid of a meaningful economic analysis of the cause of the war fosters the illusion that the antiwar movement by itself will be able to pressure the U.S. out of Vietnam. The notion that simply more activism and more protesters can end the war is an essentially pacifist proposition; such an unrealistic and anti-political approach is a dangerous conservative barrier to the political understanding and development of the antiwar movement.

Revolutionary Marxists should be helping the antiwar movement find the correct road to political unity by demonstrating the necessity of independent anti-capitalist politics that connect the war to the other evils of the system. Political ventures that stop short of such a program are doomed to capitulation to the Democratic Party and to class-collaboration politics.

Vanguard elements of the antiwar movement feel their isolation from the working class to be a basic weakness of the movement, and they seek alliances with the proletariat and specifically with Negroes, that section of the working class already in motion. As a consequence of a serious effort to stop the war, antiwar militants are groping for fundamental solutions to social problems. They seek to unite Negroes, the poverty-stricken, draft resisters, radical unionists, socialists, and rebellious youth into a broad political movement. Revolutionaries are obligated to help them find their way.

It must be patiently explained that the capitalist class has a fundamental stake in this particular war and will not quit short of military/political defeat in Vietnam or virtual civil war at home.

III. Organizational principles

(1) For internal democracy

We adhere to the principle of a living democratic centralism.

This means an elected leadership responsible to the membership, majority rule, unity in action, free and critical internal discussion and debate, and guaranteed minority rights. This means a toleration of differences and a respect for discipline—the interpenetration of individuality and solidarity.

(2) For an independent socialist youth movement

The need of young rebels for organizational independence and autonomy greatly facilitates the development of a virile cadre of young socialists who will constitute the decisive contingent of tomorrow's leadership.

There is a great promise in this direction.

Perspectives

In stark contrast to the conservative and relatively quiescent white working class stand the Negro freedom fighters. Their demands express the historic needs of the working class as a whole in the struggle against capitalist exploitation. Predominantly workers, Negroes comprise an objectively revolutionary force, for the status quo is intolerable to them now and yet their most elementary demands cannot be won within the present social system.

The existence of this potentially revolutionary mass force within the context of an approaching general economic crisis indicates that the coming period in the U.S. will be pre-revolutionary.

The impact of Negro radicalism has thus far primarily jarred youth, radicals, women, students and the churches. But as the leadership of the movement matures, a chain reaction occurs in the working class.

The coming mass radicalization will be accompanied by a regeneration of revolutionary thought and a massive reorganization of the socialist vanguard. These are the indispensable elements for the victory of the American Revolution.

Notes

1   Jack Barnes, "Leading the Party into Industry," (Report to the SWP National Committee, February 24, 1978), *The Changing Face of U.S. Politics,* 2nd ed. (New York: Pathfinder, 1994), p. 133.

2   *A Victory for Socialist Feminism: Organizer's Report to the 1969 FSP Conference,* 2nd ed. (Seattle: Freedom Socialist Party Publications, 1976). Gloria Martin, *Socialist Feminism: The First Decade, 1966-76,* 2nd ed. (Seattle: Freedom Socialist Publications, 1986).

3   Hans Magnus Enzensberger (1929 -), Germany's foremost modern poet and literary critic, gave up his fellowship at Ohio's Wesleyan University and moved to Cuba for a year in protest against the Vietnam War. His caustic criticism of U.S. foreign policy and praise for Cuba were published in the *New York Times.*

4   The Smith Act (officially titled the Alien Registration Act) was passed by Congress in 1940. It provided severe prison sentences for "teaching or advocating the overthrow of the United States government by force or violence" or for conspiring to do so. The first political victims of the Smith Act were 18 Socialist Workers Party leaders—indicted in 1941 and imprisoned in 1944 for opposing President Roosevelt's imperialist war policies. The Communist Party supported the prosecution because of its virulent hostility to the Trotskyist opponents of Stalin and because it endorsed U.S. involvement in World War II. However, in 1949, eleven Communist Party leaders were also jailed under Smith Act provisions. In 1957, the U.S. Supreme Court restricted the Smith Act to actions rather than ideas, which made further successful prosecutions difficult. See James P. Cannon, *Socialism on Trial,* 5th ed. (New York: Pathfinder Press, 1973) and James P. Cannon, *Letters from Prison* (New York: Merit Publishers, 1968).

5   David Dreiser was a member of the Los Angeles branch of the SWP in the 1940s and later worked with the SWP's New York branch. A collaborator with Richard Fraser in developing the Revolutionary Integration analysis of the African American struggle, Dreiser resigned from the SWP in 1966 along with the Seattle branch.

6   The Third International, also known as the Communist Interna-

tional or Comintern, was founded in 1919 by Lenin and other Bolshevik leaders to coordinate the efforts of Communist parties around the world. Under Stalin, the Comintern became a rubber-stamp for the Soviet bureaucracy's policy of accommodation to world capitalism. The Third International was disbanded by Stalin in 1943. Although it no longer existed as a body when *Crisis and Leadership* was written, the Stalinist forces that had comprised the International were still the major barrier to world revolution, but were also undergoing a shake-up due to the impact of the Chinese Revolution.

7   "Permanent Revolution" is the Trotskyist concept that the liberation struggles of oppressed people, classes and nations are an unstoppable, constantly unfolding, interconnected, international process which, under the conditions of modern imperialism, can only be won through a socialist revolution.

8   During the late 1950s and early '60s, relations between China and the Soviet Union degenerated to the point of possible warfare between the two workers states. The conflict, known as the Sino-Soviet dispute, grew out of the economic disparity between the two countries and their different positions toward world imperialism. The USSR followed the Stalinist policy of peaceful co-existence with the capitalist world, while China, fearful of imperialist invasion, looked for support to the emerging Third World. China's vituperation against the Soviet Union eventually led it into the arms of the United States which it saw as a lesser enemy than the Soviets.

9   W.E.B. DuBois (1868-1963) was a brilliant African American intellectual, prolific writer, and civil rights fighter. He became increasingly radical during his life, starting out as a leader of the NAACP and later blending Pan-Africanism with Marxism. Harassed by the government during the 1950s for his associations with leftists, DuBois defiantly and publicly joined the Communist Party and then moved to Ghana. He became a citizen of Ghana in 1961.

10   "Dual power" is a Marxist term explained by Trotsky in *The History of the Russian Revolution* and elsewhere. It is a symptom of a society in a pre-revolutionary condition in which the state institutions of the revolutionary class have a high degree of development and confront the old institutions with a competing or "dual" state power. For example, the Committees of Public Safety in both the American and French revolutions existed for a considerable time side-by-side with the state institutions of the old order, objectively preparing for insurrection.

11   The Compromise of 1877 was the infamous horse-trade between the Democratic and Republican parties which ended Reconstruction by giving the Republicans the presidency in return

for unhampered terroristic rule of the South by the Democrats.

12 In April 1963, the Southern Christian Leadership Conference (SCLC) launched a massive campaign of demonstrations, civil disobedience, boycotts and sit-ins in Birmingham, Alabama, one of the most segregated cities in the country. Police Commissioner Eugene "Bull" Connor ordered police to attack the demonstrators with clubs, police dogs and fire hoses. Over 2,500 were jailed. On May 10, an agreement was reached to end the protests in exchange for desegregation of public facilities, increased hiring of Blacks, and the release of jailed demonstrators. To stop the agreement, white supremacists went on a violent rampage against the Black community. On the night of May 11, bombs destroyed the home of Rev. A.D. King (brother of Rev. Martin Luther King, Jr.) and the Gaston Motel, headquarters of the desegregation campaign. Thousands of Blacks took to the streets throughout the night, pelting police and state troopers with rocks and bottles and burning white businesses. On the following day, 250 state troopers were sent in and President Kennedy put 3,000 federal troops on standby.

13 The John Birch Society is a fanatically anti-communist rightwing organization named for John Birch (1918-1945), a Baptist missionary and Air Force intelligence officer who was killed in China. Founded in December 1958, its membership soared after the defeat of Senator Goldwater's 1964 presidential campaign. By 1967, the Society had a paid staff, nearly 80,000 members in 4,000 chapters nationwide, and a budget estimated at $20 million dollars.

14 The House Un-American Activities Committee (HUAC) is the most well-known of numerous inquisitorial anti-communist legislative committees in state and federal government during the 1950s. Formed in 1938, HUAC became an immensely powerful, permanent committee of the House of Representatives mandated to investigate "subversive and un-American propaganda activities." See David Caute, *The Great Fear: The Anti-Communist Purge Under Truman and Eisenhower* (New York: Simon & Schuster, 1978).

15 Barry Morris Goldwater (1909-1998), a wealthy heir from Arizona, was an architect of the conservative revival in the Republican Party in the 1950s and '60s. He was the unsuccessful 1964 Republican presidential candidate against Lyndon B. Johnson. In accepting the Republican nomination, he declared, "Extremism in the defense of liberty is no vice, and moderation in the pursuit of justice is no virtue."

16 The reference to SWP blindness to "nonclassical" fascism alludes to the prevailing attitude in the SWP that the Goldwater movement could not be fascist in nature because it did not ap-

pear to be directed against the labor movement.

17 Robert F. Williams (1925-1996) mobilized armed self-defense against Klan violence in 1957 as head of the Monroe, North Carolina chapter of the NAACP. A year later, he and the SWP's Committee to Combat Racial Injustice organized a successful international campaign to free two Black boys, ages 7 and 9, who were imprisoned for rape after one boy allowed a white playmate to kiss his check. In 1961, Williams and four others were indicted on trumped-charges of "kidnapping" a white couple in the midst of tense confrontations between white mobs and Monroe's African American community. Williams and his wife, Mabel, fled to Cuba and later China. They returned to the U.S. in 1969 and charges were finally dropped in 1976. See Robert F. Williams, *Negroes with Guns,* (New York: Marzani & Munsell, 1962); Truman Nelson, *People with Strength: The Story of Monroe, N.C.* (New York: Marzani & Munsell, [1962]); and August Meier, editor, *Black Protest Thought in the Twentieth Century* (New York: Bobbs-Merrill, 1971), 361-372.

James Boggs (1919 -), an auto worker and political theorist, was active in the SWP in the late '40s. He and his wife, Grace Lee Boggs, were part of the Johnsonite Tendency in the SWP which included the West Indian author C.L.R. James (J.R. Johnson) and Raya Dunayevskaya. James Boggs is the author of *The American Revolution: Pages from a Negro Worker's Notebook* (New York: Monthly Review Press, 1963) and *Racism and the Class Struggle: Further Pages from a Black Worker's Notebook* (New York: Monthly Review Press, 1971).

Bill Epton was Vice-Chairman of the Progressive Labor Party and Chairman of its Harlem branch. In 1964, he was charged with "criminal anarchy" for defying a ban on protests and calling a march to denounce the police murder of a 15-year-old Black youth. The case triggered an intense Grand Jury witch-hunt of the student and radical movement. Epton was convicted and sentenced to a year in jail. Progressive Labor Party, a 1962 split from the Communist Party, was militant, youth-oriented, and critical of the CP's reformist politics, but was also Stalinist.

Fanny Lou Hamer (1917-1977), a 47-year-old sharecropper from Ruleville, Mississippi, lost her home and livelihood in 1962 after attempting to register to vote. She became a field secretary for the Student Non-Violent Coordinating Committee (SNCC). In 1963, after being arrested at the Winona, Mississippi bus station, Hamer and three other Black women activists were viciously beaten in their jail cells. Hamer was a founder and Vice-Chairman of the Mississippi Freedom Democratic Party (MFDP), which challenged the white-controlled Democratic Party at the ballot box and national party conventions. See Kay

Mills, *This Little Light of Mine: The Life of Fannie Lou Hamer* (New York: Dutton, 1993).

Victoria Jackson Gray, of Hattiesburg, Mississippi, was on the board of directors of the Southern Christian Leadership Conference, a director of its voter registration drive, a schoolteacher and businesswoman. In June 1964, she and Fanny Lou Hamer became the first African American women in Mississippi to run for Congress, as part of a slate of five Mississippi Freedom Democratic Party candidates. Gray was elected National Committeewoman of the MFDP at its 1964 convention.

18   The Monroe Doctrine, articulated by President James Monroe in 1823, declared North and South America off-limits to European colonization. As a linchpin of United States foreign policy, it has been used many times to justify U.S. invasions throughout the Americas, and was invoked on April 28, 1965 by President Lyndon B. Johnson when he sent U.S. troops "to prevent the spread of communism" by crushing the revolution in the Dominican Republic.

19   Reconstruction (1865-1877) is the period following the American Civil War during which Blacks voted and held office in Southern states and endeavored to build new institutions of equality, universal suffrage and education, and advanced social programs. Reconstruction was defeated by Ku Klux Klan terror and a back room deal known as the Compromise of 1877, in which Democrats gave the presidency to the Republicans in exchange for withdrawal of all federal troops and oversight in the South. Civil rights for African Americans were lost for another 100 years. See W.E.B. DuBois, *Black Reconstruction in America, 1860-1880* (New York: Atheneum, 1977).

20   The Mississippi Freedom Democratic Party directly confronted the pro-segregation southern Democratic Party. It ran opposition candidates and staged independent Freedom elections where it was denied ballot status. At the 1964 National Democratic Convention, the MFDP demanded to be seated in place of the Democratic delegation which had been selected without Black participation. Moderates such as Martin Luther King, Jr. and Roy Wilkins urged a compromise brokered by President Johnson and Senator Hubert H. Humphrey that would grant only special at-large status to two MFDP representatives. Fannie Lou Hamer spoke out against the compromise and the delegates unanimously rejected it. Hamer led a nationally televised demonstration on the convention floor and the MFDP walked out. At the 1968 Democratic Party convention, the MFDP joined a coalition of integrationists, white liberals, the NAACP, and the state AFL-CIO in a successful challenge to the regular Democratic Party delegation from Mississippi.

21 Populism originated in the 1870s as an anti-Big Business, anti-authoritarian movement of U.S. farmers. As the Populist Party, or Peoples' Party, founded in 1892, it was often successful in forming coalitions between Black laborers and white farmers. The Democratic Party and white power structure used racism and violence to keep white farmers and farm laborers from allying with the Populist Party in the South. In 1896, the party disappeared into the Democratic Party. A century later, the label of populism has been adopted both by liberals such as Jim Hightower and his newspaper, the *Progressive Populist,* and by the far right, whose Populist Party is an electoral vehicle of the U.S. fascist movement.

22 "Freedom Now: The New Stage in the Struggle for Negro Emancipation and the Tasks of the SWP," Draft Resolution presented by the Political Committee to the 1963 SWP National Convention, *SWP Information Bulletin,* Vol. 24, No. 13, (1963). Elijah Muhammad (1897-1975) was the founder and leader of the conservative, super-nationalist Nation of Islam or Black Muslims. Malcolm X (1925-1965) had been the most prominent spokesperson of the Muslims, but when he publicly broke with Elijah Muhammad and adopted a program of revolutionary, multiracial internationalism, he was murdered by a member of the Muslims.

23 Frank H. Little (1879-1917): Son of a Cherokee mother and a Quaker father, Little was a metal miner and a founder of the Industrial Workers of the World (IWW). He gained renown as an agitator, labor organizer and free speech fighter throughout the West. Unlike the IWW leadership, Little opposed American intervention in World War I and advocated draft resistance. He was brutally murdered on August 1, 1917 while organizing a miners' strike against the Anaconda Company in Butte, Montana. His killers were never found. See James P. Cannon, *Notebook of an Agitator,* 2nd ed. (New York: Pathfinder Press, 1973).

Medgar Wiley Evers (1925-1963): A Mississippi-born civil rights activist, Evers became the NAACP's first State Field-Secretary (1954). He organized boycotts of Jackson, Mississippi merchants, traveled throughout the state teaching parents how to file school-desegregation petitions, and investigated the lynching of 14-year-old Emmett Till and the killings of several civil rights workers. In 1962, with NAACP backing, Evers encouraged James Meredith (1933 -) to enroll at the all-white University of Mississippi at Oxford. In 1963, while leading a major desegregation drive in Jackson, Evers was shot in the back and killed. His murderer was caught but set free twice by deadlocked all-white juries in the 1960s. In 1994, a third trial finally convicted white supremacist Byron de la Beckwith and sentenced him to life in prison. See Maryanne Vollers, *Ghosts of Mississippi: The Murder of Medgar Evers, the Trials of Byron de la Beckwith, and the Haunting of the New South* (Boston: Little, Brown, 1995).

24 *The Protocols of Zion* (also known as *The Protocols of the Elders of Zion*) is a classic pamphlet of anti-Semitism written in the 1890s. It is a false account of the first Zionist congress and claims to expose a plot by a group of rabbis to manipulate governments and take control of world finance. It has been translated into most major languages, and is widely sold by rightwing extremists.

25 Albert Buford Cleage, Jr. (1911- 2000), pastor of a Detroit church, was a member of the NAACP Executive Board. He was a conservative, nationalistic force within the Freedom Now Party in Michigan, which he served as State Chairman and gubernatorial candidate in 1964. He later became an advocate for Christianity as a "liberating force" in his books *Black Messiah* (New York: Sheed and Ward, 1968) and *Black Christian Nationalism: New Directions for the Black Church* (New York: W. Morrow, 1972).

26 In January 1965, Malcolm X sent a telegram to George Lincoln Rockwell, head of the American Nazi Party: "This is to warn you that I am no longer held in check from fighting white supremacists by Elijah Muhammad's separatist Black Muslim movement...that you and your Ku Klux Klan friends will be met with maximum physical retaliation from those of us who are not handcuffed by the disarming philosophy of nonviolence, and who believe in asserting our right to self-defense—by any means necessary." Malcolm X, *Malcolm X Speaks: Selected Speeches and Statements,* 2nd ed. (New York: Pathfinder Press, 1989), p. 201.

27 Daniel Guérin (1904-1988), a French writer and revolutionary theorist, lived in the United States from 1946-49 and wrote a seminal study of the Black liberation struggle, *Negroes on the March: A Frenchman's Report on the American Negro Struggle* (New York: Weissman, 1956). He is also the author of an important work on fascism, *Fascism and Big Business,* 2nd ed. (New York: Monad Press, 1973). Guérin had links with Trotsky but disagreed with him over the creation of the Fourth International. In the 1970s and '80s, he attempted to reconcile Marxism with anarchism in what he termed "libertarian communism" and became an activist for gay rights.

28 Rev. Martin Luther King, Jr. and Roy Wilkins represented the moderate wing of the civil rights struggle. Rev. King (1929-1968), from Atlanta, Georgia, rose to national prominence when he was chosen to lead the 1956 Montgomery, Alabama bus boycott to end segregation on the city's buses. (See note 33.) He

served as head of the Southern Christian Leadership Conference from 1957 until his death. An advocate of nonviolence, King was awarded the Nobel Peace prize in 1964. He was assassinated on April 3, 1968, while assisting with a strike in Memphis, Tennessee.

Roy Wilkins (1901-1981) led the NAACP from 1931-1977. He believed that racial equality could be achieved through legalistic means rather than direct action.

29 Three years after the authors described the course of northern "nationalists" and southern "integrationists" as being an identical trajectory toward socialism, Huey Newton, Black Panther Party Minister of Defense, stated in an interview in a SNCC publication, "To be a revolutionary nationalist, you would by necessity have to be a socialist." *The Movement,* Volume 4 (August 1968), monthly publication of the Student Nonviolent Coordinating Committee, published in San Francisco.

30 William Worthy (1921 -) was a groundbreaking African American foreign correspondent for CBS television news. In the 1950s and '60s, he defied U.S. travel bans and seizure of his passport to report on events from inside China, Cuba, North Vietnam, Cambodia and Indonesia.

The Freedom Now Party was formally launched on August 28, 1963 at the March on Washington and in Black communities in Detroit, Chicago, Cleveland, San Francisco, Los Angeles, New York, Seattle, and other cities. The first acting chairman was Conrad J. Lynn, a veteran African American civil rights lawyer whose cases included the Monroe, North Carolina "Kissing Case" (see note 17) and defense of revolutionary Puerto Rican nationalists. After running candidates in New York, Connecticut, and California in the 1963 elections, the party decided to concentrate efforts in only one state, Michigan, the following year. Under the leadership of Michigan State Chairman Albert Cleage (see note 25), the party ran 39 Black candidates for local, state and federal offices in 1964.

31 "The Marseillaise" is the rousing national anthem of France, written in 1792.

32 A People's Front is an unprincipled, cross-class alliance which seeks to attract the largest number of people possible on the basis of a diluted program under the leadership of pro-capitalist liberals and reformists. The concept was developed by the Comintern in 1935 to justify subordination of workers interests in coalition governments with liberal bourgeois parties, for example, the Popular Front governments in France and Spain in 1936.

In contrast, Trotskyists pose the tactic of the United Front: a coalition of organizations based on a workingclass program that agrees to work together on a particular issue such as fighting fascism, while reserving the right to disagree on other subjects.

33 On December 1, 1955, Rosa Parks (1913 -), a seamstress, secretary of the local NAACP chapter, and a respected figure in the Black community of Montgomery, Alabama, refused to give up her seat on the bus to a white man. She was arrested and jailed. The following day, the Women's Political Council, led by Jo Ann Gibson Robinson, called for a boycott of the buses and enlisted the support of Montgomery clergymen, including Dr. Martin Luther King, Jr. Under the leadership of King and the Montgomery Improvement Association, the boycott continued for 382 days and finally won a federal Supreme Court order requiring integration of Montgomery's buses. See Jo Ann Gibson Robinson, *The Montgomery Bus Boycott and the Women Who Started It* (Knoxville: University of Tennessee Press, 1987).

34 In the period after this was written, Black women were consciously forced out of positions of leadership in the liberation movement. This represented a retreat for the movement. There is little that is revolutionary in the fight against "emasculation" and for male supremacy. Such a struggle can only represent the interests of a nascent Black bourgeoisie, trying to incorporate itself into the existing social order—at the expense of the great mass of Black Americans, male and female.

35 For information on Southern white women's resistance to white supremacy, see Lillian Smith, *Killers of the Dream*, rev. ed. (New York: Norton, 1978).

36 Gloria Richardson (1922 -) led a desegregation campaign in Cambridge, Maryland in 1963-1964, which mobilized nonviolent demonstrations during the day and armed resistance by night to protect the town's 4,200 Blacks from the population of 8,000 whites. Arrested three times and shot at twice, Richardson also successfully fought two attempts by whites to commit her to a mental institution. In August 1964, in the midst of the struggle, she resigned as chair of the Cambridge Non-Violent Action Committee and dropped out to get married. Although she had been the first woman in the country to lead a major Black protest movement, Richardson lacked confidence in herself as a leader. She said, "When I get on the platform...and the men are all there, I just feel there is nothing more to say." In the '70s, Richardson became active in the National Council of Negro Women in New York City. See John D'Emilio, *The Civil Rights Struggle: Leaders in Profile* (New York: Facts on File, 1979), p. 124; and "Whatever Happened to Gloria Richardson?," *Ebony*, Number 29 (February 1974): 138.

37 Frederick Engels, *Origin of the Family, Private Property and the*

State (New York: International Publishers, 1972), p. 221.

38 Daniel De Leon, "Translator's Preface," to August Bebel, *Woman Under Socialism* (New York: Schocken Books, 1971), p. xv.

39 Karl Marx, *Capital,* Vol. 1 (New York: International Publishers, 1967), p. 460.

40 Frederick Engels, *Origin of the Family, Private Property and the State* (New York: International Publishers, 1972), p. 137-138.

41 The film *Salt of the Earth* was based on a 17-month strike by Chicano and Mexicano zinc miners in Silver City, New Mexico in 1950-51. An injunction against the male strikers moved their wives to take over the picket lines—sparking their evolution from men's subordinates into their equals and allies. The film was made during the height of the McCarthy era by a group of blacklisted filmmakers with support from the union which had led the strike, the International Union of Mine, Mill and Smelter Workers. Though *Salt of the Earth* was boycotted by U.S. movie theaters because of its politics, it won many international awards and is now among 100 films selected by the Library of Congress to be preserved for posterity.

42 Jim Crow locals were segregated or discriminatory union locals that allowed African Americans to become members but gave them little protection. Despite their union status, they remained the last hired and first fired, and were relegated to the worst jobs.

43 "Operation Dixie" was an ambitious organizing campaign launched by the CIO in May 1946 with the goal of recruiting a million southern workers to the CIO. It failed within two years due to the CIO's unwillingness to break with the Democratic Party which ran the southern police state and was a pillar of white supremacy. Art Preis, *Labor's Giant Step: Twenty Years of the CIO,* 2nd ed. (New York: Pathfinder Press, 1972), p. 376-377.

44 The Wagner Act (the National Labor Relations Act of 1935) legitimized the existence of unions, set up procedures for seeking union recognition, legalized strikes, and established the National Labor Relations Board (NLRB) to mediate between unions and management. The act is named for the prominent New Deal advocate and U.S. Senator from New York, Robert F. Wagner.

45 The original Kirk-Kaye resolution ended with a discussion of "Tasks of the SWP," which the authors did not revise for a public audience. Instead, coauthor Clara Fraser viewed Part Two of this book, "Radical Laborism versus Bolshevik Leadership," as the companion piece to the preceding sections of *Crisis and Leadership.*

46 The Cochranites were an unprincipled combination of revision-

ists within the SWP. The grouping, led by Bert Cochran (1917-1981), was mainly affected by regressive moods among trade unionists. They became party liquidationists, skeptical of any need for an active revolutionary vanguard. This group aligned itself with George Clarke and Milton Zaslow (often referred to by his pseudonym Mike Bartell), who were both advocates of the thinking of Michel Pablo (pseudonym of Greek socialist Michel Raptis), a leader of the Fourth International. Pablo predicted that centuries of degenerated, Stalinist-controlled workers states were the prospect for the future, rendering Trotskyism irrelevant for an entire historic period. Clarke and Bartell were also liquidationists who demanded the entry of U.S. Trotskyists into Stalinist-led movements and organizations. After a bitter faction fight, the Cochranite minority was expelled in 1953 for refusing to respect party discipline. The Cochran tendency dissolved shortly thereafter.

47   Farrell Dobbs (1907-1983) was a leader of the famous Minneapolis Teamster strikes and the Teamsters union in the 1930s. He subsequently became National Secretary of the SWP. Tom Kerry (1899-1982) joined the SWP in the '30s, gained experience with agricultural and maritime workers, and became a fixture of the SWP's National Office staff.

48   Murry Weiss (1915-1981) and Myra Tanner Weiss (1917-1997) represented a tendency within the SWP that was characterized by an emphasis on political theory, an activist and interventionist approach to strategy and tactics, and commitment to the Woman Question as a needed component of party principles and practice. They had an enviable record of building leadership cadres of professional revolutionaries. Among those they trained was Freedom Socialist Party founder Clara Fraser (1923-1998). Myra Tanner Weiss joined the SWP in 1935 and became a dynamic and highly respected organizer-leader. She was the SWP's foremost female spokesperson and three-time candidate for U.S. vice-president. She organized the Young Socialist Alliance, the SWP youth group, with Murry Weiss, a founding member and longtime leader, political analyst and creative organizer of the SWP. The Weisses left the SWP in the 1960s. In the 1970s, they made contact with Clara Fraser and the Freedom Socialist Party, and in 1977, the FSP, the Weisses and other Trotskyists outside the SWP formed a regroupment vehicle called Committee for a Revolutionary Socialist Party. Murry Weiss joined the FSP in 1979.

49   The Fair Play for Cuba Committee, which the SWP was instrumental in launching and leading, was dissolved in 1963 following the Kennedy assassination. Founded in 1960, it was the only U.S. organization to publicly defend, support and explain the

1959 Cuban Revolution. Ever since the revolution, the U.S. State Department has stringently prohibited travel to Cuba and placed an embargo on trade, humanitarian assistance, and other forms of exchange with the country.

50   The *Militant* is the weekly newspaper of the SWP. The *National Guardian,* later the *Guardian*, was a long-lived, independent radical weekly which folded in 1990. *Weekly People,* now the *People,* is the newspaper published by the Socialist Labor Party, a Marxist, but anti-Leninist group founded in 1877 in the U.S. by Daniel DeLeon.

51   Political Resolution: "The Next Phase of American Politics," Political Committee Draft Resolution, *SWP Internal Information Bulletin* 25, no. 2 (1965). Organizational Resolution: "The Organizational Character of the SWP," Draft Resolution Adopted by the January 1965 Plenum of the National Committee, *SWP Internal Information Bulletin* 25, no. 3 (1965).

52   The Committee to Aid the Monroe Defendants raised bail and provided legal defense for Robert Williams and other victims of a racist frame-up in Monroe, North Carolina. (See note 17.)

53   The petty-bourgeois opposition known as the Shachtmanite faction, developed within the SWP on the eve of WWII. In reaction to pro-war, patriotic sentiments, the Shachtmanites opposed Trotsky's policy of unconditional defense of the Soviet workers state against imperialist attack. The faction, led by Max Shachtman (1903-1972), James Burnham (1905-1987) and Martin Abern (1898-1949), called the USSR "state capitalist" or "bureaucratic collectivist." This unprincipled bloc, which spanned diverse political positions, also repudiated dialectical materialism, challenged James P. Cannon's leadership and methods, and demanded a separate public journal to promote their minority viewpoint. After a bitter and protracted battle, they were expelled in 1940 for violating party discipline. For a complete account of the faction struggle, see James P. Cannon, *The Struggle for a Proletarian Party,* 2nd ed. (New York: Pathfinder Press, 1973) and Leon Trotsky, *In Defense of Marxism*, 2nd ed. (New York: Pathfinder Press, 1973).

54   Economism was a tendency among early Russian "Marxists" who advocated pure and simple trade unionism, i.e., exclusive attention by the unions to bread-and-butter economic questions. Lenin denounced this separation of revolutionary political work from economic issues within the unions, insisting that the struggle against employers be connected with the anti-government struggle. See V.I. Lenin, *What is to be Done?* (New York: International Publishers, 1969). The Dobbs-Kerry policy was similarly nonpolitical in the labor movement, as well as non-proletarian in the other mass movements.

55 Leon Trotsky advanced the concept of a sliding scale of working hours and wages to unify workers in the struggle against rising prices and increasing unemployment. While "30 for 40" is a progressive reform that is achievable under capitalism, the sliding scale of wages and hours exposes the capitalists' utter inability and unwillingness to guarantee livable conditions for workers in time of economic crisis. See Leon Trotsky, *The Transitional Program for Socialist Revolution* (New York: Pathfinder Press, 1973), p. 47, 77.

56 The "Third Camp" is composed of those who reject both capitalism and the workers states, thereby abstaining from the class struggle. At the outset of the Korean War (1950-53), the SWP asserted a policy of neutrality instead of opposing U.S. aggression against the North Korean workers state. When warships embarked for Korea from Seattle, Dan Roberts, Clara Fraser, and other members of the Seattle SWP issued a press release denouncing U.S. intervention. They also picketed the Navy's waterfront piers. Upon proudly informing the SWP National Office of their actions, they were reprimanded for violating policy because the SWP was taking "no position" on the war. In contrast to such abstentionism is the strategy of revolutionary neutrality in which workers' parties do not take sides on an armed struggle between imperialists unless a workers state is under assault or the rights of an oppressed nation are being violated.

57 The Cuban missile crisis was provoked by President Kennedy's reckless challenge to the USSR over supposed Soviet missiles in Cuba. Soviet Premier Khrushchev withdrew from the confrontation in a last-minute concession, preventing nuclear holocaust.

58 After the assassination of President Kennedy, Dobbs went so far as to send an official letter of condolence to his widow, Jacqueline Kennedy, and the *Militant*, voice of the SWP, printed it on the front page.

59 B.J. Field was an SWP member and intellectual who, as a result of implementing party policy, achieved great prominence in the New York hotel strike of 1934. Thereupon he lost his head, believed his press notices, and proceeded to operate individualistically and unilaterally, committing serious errors all the way. He was expelled from the party in the middle of the strike. See James P. Cannon, *The History of American Trotskyism,* 2nd ed. (New York: Pathfinder Press, 1972), p. 126-134.

60 Joseph Zack (1897-1963), a brief convert from the Stalinist bureaucracy to the SWP, began to attack the party the moment he joined. After considerable disruption of party discipline, he was expelled and became a social democrat. After 1945, he became extremely right wing and frequently testified against Communists before Congressional investigating committees. See James

P. Cannon, *The History of American Trotskyism,* 2nd ed. (Pathfinder Press, 1972), p. 201-202.

61 Hugo Oehler (1903-1983) and his supporters in the U.S. Trotskyist organization took an ultra-left, sectarian position against Trotsky's strategy known as the "French Turn," in which Trotskyists in France, the U.S., and elsewhere, entered leftward-moving Socialist parties. In November 1935, after a bitter faction fight, the Oehlerites were expelled from the party. See James P. Cannon, *The History of American Trotskyism,* 2nd ed. (New York: Pathfinder Press, 1972), p. 195-198, 200-203, 214-217.

62 Martin Abern, one of the leaders of the 1939-40 Shachtmanite petty-bourgeois opposition, was an inveterate unprincipled politician, absorbed with organizational and personal gossip and always ready to combine with anyone on secondary administrative questions. His specialty was disseminating scandal about the Cannon regime. See James P. Cannon, *The Struggle for a Proletarian Party* (New York: Pathfinder Press, 1972), p. 35-49.

63 In 1945, Felix Morrow (1906 -), author of the classic history *Revolution and Counterrevolution in Spain* (New York: Pathfinder Press, 1974), joined with Albert Goldman (1897-1960) in fomenting a faction fight over similar issues to those previously raised by the Shachtmanites. The small and cynical Goldman-Morrow minority, concentrated almost exclusively in the Chicago and New York branches, was demoralized by the failure of the Western European proletariat to seize power after WWII. The faction was expelled at the 1946 SWP National Convention for violating party discipline. Morrow became a zealous anticommunist and publisher of books on the occult.

64 The Control Commission was supposed to be a small body of highly respected and responsible comrades who were *not* members of the National Committee. Commission members ordinarily were elected to the position at party conventions. Their function was to personally investigate and evaluate complex disputes and questions of discipline within the party, and report their findings and decisions to the leadership.

In the Milwaukee branch case, used the Control Commission to interfere with and reverse a valid disciplinary measure adopted by the branch against a member who stole party equipment. The Commissioners who conducted the investigation were mainly non-elected appointees who shared the regime's hostility to the Milwaukee branch because it had taken a minority position on a number of political issues.

65 Jim Robertson and Tim Wohlforth were leaders of the leftwing youth in the Socialist Party when they were recruited to the SWP by Murry Weiss in the mid-1950s. They were experienced jour-

nalists and organizers, but were also inveterate factionalists, even though their position on key issues such as the nature of the Soviet state and the Cuban Revolution shifted frequently. Dobbs and Kerry, in their hunger to "get" the Weisses, frequently concluded unprincipled organizational blocs with Wohlforth. Robertson eventually split from Wohlforth in 1963 and organized his own faction. He was expelled in 1963 and Wohlforth in 1964.

Wohlforth formed the Workers League, which was affiliated with Gerry Healy (see note 46), leader of the intensely sectarian British group, Workers Revolutionary Party. After being spurned by both organizations, Wohlforth rejoined the SWP in 1975 for a final four-year stint. See Tim Wohlforth, *The Prophet's Children: Travels on the American Left* (New Jersey: Humanities Press, 1994).

Robertson is head of the Spartacist League, an ultraleft group that specializes in irrational vituperation against other radicals. In 1967, Robertson attempted an organizational raid on the young Freedom Socialist Party. His maneuvers thoroughly deceived Richard Fraser (1913-1988) and Frank Krasnowsky, but were repudiated and condemned by the FSP majority. Dick Fraser and Krasnowsky later split from the FSP. See *A Victory for Socialist Feminism: Organizer's Report to the 1969 FSP Conference*, 2nd ed. (Seattle: Freedom Socialist Party Publications, 1976).

66   Arne Swabeck (1890-1986), a participant in the 1919 Seattle General Strike, was one of the SWP's Old Guard. A founder of the CP and SWP, he was a leading writer and theoretician. He dissented from the SWP majority over the question of the Chinese Revolution. He supported the major policies of Mao and considered Maoism to be close to Trotskyism. He was expelled from the party in 1967.

67   Nathan Gould (1913 -) and Albert Glotzer (1908-1999) left the SWP in the 1940 Shachtman-Abern split.

68   Sam Marcy was the organizer of the SWP's Buffalo branch and the leader of a cult-faction with very mechanical concepts that frequently bordered on Stalinism. The Marcyites split from the SWP in 1959 and organized the Workers World Party and Youth Against War and Fascism.

69   Gerry Healy (1913-1989), longtime leader of British Trotskyism and the Workers Revolutionary Party, collaborated with Cannon in the 1953-54 fight against Pabloism in the Fourth International (see note 46). In later years, Healy became increasingly sectarian and erratic. He was aligned with Wohlforth-Robertson in opposition to reunification of the International in 1964. Both later broke with him. In the mid-70s, Healy launched a slander

campaign against SWP leader Joseph Hansen (1911-1979) and the entire SWP leadership, calling them double-agents of the CIA and the Kremlin. Healy was expelled by the Workers Revolutionary Party in 1985 after a sex scandal. He and a few of his followers, including actor Vanessa Redgrave and her brother Colin, continued together in a grouping currently known as the Marxist Party.

70 Robert Vernon, "Why White Radicals are Incapable of Understanding Black Nationalism," *SWP Internal Discussion Bulletin* 24, no. 11 (1963). Robert Vernon was the pseudonym of Robert DesVerney (1928-1995), the SWP's leading African American exponent of Black nationalist ideology. See Osborne Hart and Jeanne Tuomey, "Bob DesVerney: Four Decades in the Fight for Communism, a Life Worth Emulating," *Militant* 59, no. 42 (November 13, 1995): 7-11.

71 Richard Kirk [Fraser], "Revolutionary Integration: Draft Resolution on the Negro Struggle," *SWP Discussion Bulletin* 24, no. 28 (June 1963), p. 40. This resolution has been republished as "Revolutionary Integration: The Dialectics of Black Liberation," Rev. ed., two-part Special Supplement to *Freedom Socialist* 3, nos. 3 and 4 (Fall and Winter 1977).

72 Hedda Garza, "An Answer to M.T. Weiss' 'Comments'," *SWP Discussion Bulletin* 24, no. 29 (July 1963).

73 *Darkness At Noon* (New York: Macmillan, 1941) is a novel by Arthur Koestler about the Moscow Trials, in which Stalin's opponents were forced into public "confession" of sabotage against the Soviet regime and executed.

74 J.R. Johnson was the pseudonym of the famous Trinidadian author, C.L.R. James (1901-1989). He left the SWP in 1940 with the Shachtmanites, but returned to the party in 1947 and wrote the 1948 resolution on the African American struggle: "Draft Resolution on the Negro Question," *SWP Internal Information Bulletin* 10, no. 3 (1948). As part of the Johnson-Forest Tendency (F. Forest was the pseudonym of Raya Dunayevskaya), James left the party once again in 1951 over differences on the nature of the Soviet Union. C.L.R. James is author of many books including *The Black Jacobins: Toussaint L'Ouverture and the San Domingo Revolution,* 2nd rev. ed. (New York: Random House, Vintage Books, 1989) and *World Revolution 1917-1936,* 2nd rev. ed. (New Jersey: Humanities Press, 1993).

75 Franz Mehring, *Karl Marx: The Story of His Life* (Ann Arbor: University of Michigan Press, 1962), p. 483.

76 James P. Cannon, *The History of American Trotskyism* 2nd ed. (New York: Pathfinder Press, 1972), p. 28.

77 In 1964, the United Socialist Convention Committee, an elec-

toral coalition comprising the Seattle SWP, ex-CPers and other independent radicals, adopted the name Freedom Socialist Party to demonstrate their connection to the civil rights freedom struggle. Under that ballot designation, the coalition ran a slate of candidates in the Washington State elections. After the split from the SWP in 1966, the former Seattle branch took the name Freedom Socialist Party.

78 See note 71.

79 In January 1966, Castro attacked Trotskyism as "a vulgar instrument of imperialism and reaction" in a speech delivered at the Tricontinental Congress in Havana. He especially denounced an international Trotskyist tendency known as the Posadistas and Adolfo Gilly, an Argentine journalist who was active in the Mexican Posadista party, the Partido Obrero Revolucionario (Trotskista). Gilly had published several widely read articles on Cuba in the U.S. magazine, *Monthly Review*. Castro also attacked China at the conference, an act which Gilly later described as symptomatic of Cuba's alignment with the USSR in the Sino-Soviet split. See Robert J. Alexander, *International Trotskyism, 1929-1985: A Documented Analysis of the Movement* (Durham, NC: Duke University Press, 1991), p. 230-231 and Joseph Hansen, *Dynamics of the Cuban Revolution: A Marxist Appreciation* (New York: Pathfinder, 1978), p. 249-251, 315-331.

80 The National Coordinating Committee to End the War in Vietnam was a coalition of antiwar groups and individuals. The conference referred to took place in November 1965 in Washington, D.C.

81 SANE, the National Committee for a Sane Nuclear Policy, was founded in 1957 to oppose nuclear testing and armaments. Its single-issue stance attracted moderates and pacifists including Albert Schweitzer, Eleanor Roosevelt, Norman Thomas, Martin Luther King, Jr., Marlon Brando and Ruby Dee. In 1987, it became SANE/Freeze and in 1993 was renamed Peace Action.

82 The National Liberation Front (NLF), also known as the Viet Cong, was North Vietnam's army in the Vietnam War (1961-1970).

Index

Available from
RED LETTER PRESS

Voices of Color
by Yolanda Alaniz and Nellie Wong, editors
An anthology by writer-activists featuring fresh outlooks on a wide range of issues from personal identity and interracial solidarity to confronting racism, sexism and homophobia. (160 pages) ... $12.95

Revolution, She Wrote
by Clara Fraser
Essays and speeches by the fiery, hilarious, profound and refreshingly optimistic founder and leading theoretician of the Freedom Socialist Party and Radical Women. (400 pages) $17.95

Socialist Feminism: The First Decade, 1966-76
by Gloria Martin
Chronicles the formative years of the Freedom Socialist Party amid the upsurges of the 1960s and '70s. A practical guide to socialist feminist organizing. (244 pages) $8.95

Gay Resistance: The Hidden History
by Sam Deaderick and Tamara Turner
A lively and impassioned survey of the origins of sexual oppression, the contributions of lesbians and gay men, and the thousand-year struggle for homosexual freedom. (56 pages) $7.00

Revolutionary Integration: The Dialectics of Black Liberation
by Richard Fraser and Clara Fraser
Groundbreaking Marxist analysis of racism as distinct from national oppression. Examines SWP vacillations toward the civil rights and Black Power movements. *Freedom Socialist* reprint $1.00

Revolutionary Integration: Yesterday and Today
by Tom Boot
Expands and updates the analysis of Black liberation by surveying modern movement history and the impact of feminism and gay liberation. *Freedom Socialist* reprint $2.50

A Victory for Socialist Feminism
Recounts the split over defense of women leaders which took place during the FSP's first year and cemented its unique revolutionary feminist character. (56 pages, mimeographed) $2.00

Order from **RED LETTER PRESS**
409 Maynard Ave. S., Suite 201, Seattle, WA 98104

For a complete list of publications:
Phone: (206)682-0990 ● Fax (206)682-8120
E-mail: RedLetterPress@juno.com ● http://www.socialism.com